Open Access Musicology

VOLUME THREE

Open Access Musicology

VOLUME THREE

Edited by

Daniel Barolsky and Trudi Wright

Lever Press (leverpress.org) is a publisher of pathbreaking scholarship. Supported by a consortium of higher education institutions focused on, and renowned for, excellence in both research and teaching, our press is grounded on three essential commitments: to be a digitally native press, to be a peer-reviewed, open access press that charges no fees to either authors or their institutions, and to be a press aligned with the liberal arts ethos.

The complete manuscript of this work was subjected to a partly closed ("single blind") review process. For more information, please see our Peer Review Commitments and Guidelines at https://www.leverpress.org/peerreview

DOI: https://doi.org/10.3998/mpub.13006960
Print ISBN: 978-1-64315-086-4
Open access ISBN: 978-1-64315-087-1

Library of Congress Control Number: 2025930139

Published in the United States of America by Lever Press, in partnership with Michigan Publishing.

Contents

Member Institution Acknowledgments

Lever Press is a collective effort. This work was made possible by the generous support of Lever Press member libraries from the following institutions:

Amherst College
Atlanta University Center Consortium
Berea College
Bowdoin College
Carleton College
Central Washington University
Claremont Colleges
Claremont Graduate University
Claremont McKenna College
Clark Atlanta University
College of Saint Benedict & Saint John's University
The College of Wooster
Davidson College
Denison University
DePauw University
Grinnell College
Hamilton College
Hampshire College
Harvey Mudd College
Hollins University
Iowa State University
Keck Graduate Institute
Knox College
Lafayette College
Macalester College
Middlebury College
Morehouse College
Morehouse School of Medicine
Norwich University
Occidental College
Penn State University
Pitzer College

Pomona College
Randolph-Macon College
Rollins College
Santa Clara University
Scripps College
Skidmore College
Smith College
Spelman College
Susquehanna University
Swarthmore College
Trinity University
UCLA Library
Union College
University of Delaware
University of Idaho
University of Northern Colorado
University of Puget Sound
University of Rhode Island
University of San Francisco
University of Sheffield
University of Vermont
Vassar College
Washington and Lee University
Whitman College
Whittier College
Willamette University
Williams College

Preface

In his 2023 article, "What the Public Really Thinks About Higher Education," in the *Chronicle of Higher Education*, Eric Kelderman reports on a poll conducted to better understand America's perceived ambivalence toward a college education. Kelderman states:

> Most people, whether they have a four-year degree or not, would advise others to pursue one, our poll found. Yet many don't think institutions do a great job educating their students—or that they are of great benefit to graduates. […] The findings that college graduates themselves are not very impressed with the quality of their education should give colleges pause. Has the idea of college become commoditized rather than a journey of intellectual maturation as it has often been portrayed?

All those involved with *OAM* are fully committed to our students' "journeys of intellectual maturation," which is why we spend so much time and energy creating this journal. And, as much as possible, we are dedicated to an open access model disconnected from financial gain that serves the needs of college and university instructors designing courses with their students' best interests in mind.

As editors and instructors, however, we also continue to learn and grow from the challenging questions and issues that our authors present, even when that means reflecting our own practices and positions. It is not lost on us, as John Pippen's essay prompts, that, as editors, most of us do benefit from the privileges derived from institutional or academic patronage (that is, the colleges or universities that employ us), and that our labor is expected as part of our job descriptions. Indeed, both Pippen's essay and Marianna Ritchey's introduction to music and Marxism remind us that music making, consumption, and also publishing about music (such as *Open Access Musicology*!) exist within broader political and economic systems that affect what, how, where, and why music is made, performed, recorded, or even forgotten. Moreover, these systems have long and complicated histories that have influenced whose musicking is promoted and financially supported, and what strings of power shape and have shaped histories of music. All of the essays in this issue of *OAM* (and from previous issues as well) explore some aspect of gatekeeping (good, bad, and in-between), whether by record companies, courts of law, aesthetic or generic categories, or even our own moral or ethical compasses.

Katie Leo's essay on musical copyright demonstrates the deeply interconnected nature of law and judicial taste, where legal dicta can be read as musical criticism, and how these subjective opinions guide legal opinions. Stephanie Doktor's case study of the jazz band leader Fletcher Henderson explores how both jazz scholarship/criticism and the recording industries conflated spoken or unspoken connections between musical style and race that segregate musicians or promote some musics over others. In both of these histories we can see how problematic values from the past became normalized or engrained within many of the structures and systems that continue today.

Vilde Aaslid's study of Charles Mingus explores how the jazz musician challenged and reimagined the very definitions of composition and improvisation, especially when faced with previous conceptions that reinforced racialized hierarchies. Similarly, Anna Schultz's account of the kirtankar, Govindbuva Hoshing Nashikkar, examines the ways that writing about a musician's biography and history contributes to and adjusts the shifting intersection among genre, class, and religion. Moreover, Schultz demonstrates, as do many of our essays, the complicated relationship between the past and the present. This includes the ways in which the past can be reimagined as well as the ways legacies of the past are inscribed in present-day practices, structures, histories, and beliefs.

Our final essay is this issue, written collectively and responsively by Tony Perman, Deborah Wong, Putu Hiranmayena, Nkululeko Zungu, and Renata Yazzie, urges us to consider the challenges of musical futures and, in particular, the impact of our choices. We cannot change the past; but as students, performers, historians, theorists, or activists, we can learn from our histories to determine how best to play, retire, or reimagine music's role in shaping the world around us. As the authors collectively assert, the answers are varied, conflicting, and messy. Moreover, there is no single correct answer to the question they pose ("Should I perform it?"). Instead the authors encourage the readers to find it within themselves to grapple with their own identities, contexts, and motivations.

By this same token, none of our essays present complete histories of any particular music. Rather, they present provocative case studies and analyses through which readers can choose their own paths while also putting these essays in conversation with those in previous issues. Just as with any form of cultural (or culinary) omnivory, we acknowledge that our choice of ingredients and dishes remains limited. *Open Access Musicology* will never pretend to present complete histories, cover all elements of a subject, or satisfy the agenda of every reader. Instead, each essay provides an opening to further contemplation and study. We invite readers to follow the thematic links between essays, pursue notes or other online resources provided by authors, or simply repurpose the essay's questions into new and exciting forms of research and creativity.

These essays are written with a wide range of readers in mind; digital access to the volume is free of charge, thanks to the generosity of the institutions that fund Lever Press; and the essays in this collection are open to different uses. At *OAM*, it is our mission to bring undergraduate readers content that helps them along their "journey of intellectual maturation," which includes critical thinking, questioning, and analysis.

In addition, it has been our goal, from the outset, to feature essays that fit the necessary double bill of integrating cutting-edge research and scholarship in a manner and on a platform that makes such information available and accessible to undergraduate students. We're thrilled to be able to share these essays with you!

Daniel Barolsky, Editor
Trudi Wright, Editor

Acknowledgments

Open Access Musicology continues to be a labor of love. The authors, editors, and publishers do not profit from this work, although many of us are privileged to have institutional support for our time and effort. We wish to express our profound gratitude for our authors, our editorial board, and to all those who reviewed the essays in this collection. We would also like to thank the board of Lever Press for endorsing *OAM*, and the Lever editors, copyeditors, typesetters, and back-end technology specialists who support our work. We are also eternally thankful for the dozens of faculty and students who have reviewed, read, taught, and learned from our essays. We challenge all our authors to write with purpose and to remain relevant. Your responses give us hope that these essays may continue to enact positive change now and into the future.

Finally, we would like to express our gratitude to Louis Epstein, one of our founding editors, who is stepping away from much of his editorial work in order to pursue other professional passions. The journal has benefited from Louis's editorial acumen, social and political tact, professional networks, technical and commercial know-how and, above all else, his friendship and humanity. We wish you nothing but success as you continue onto new adventures, Louis!

Daniel Barolsky, Editor
Trudi Wright, Editor

CHAPTER ONE

RACIALIZING SOUND IN EARLY JAZZ

A Case Study on Fletcher Henderson (with help from Lil Nas X)

Stephanie DeLane Doktor

Growing up in an abusive household governed by a mentally ill parent, I developed a profound concern for individuals whom our society does not protect but instead exploits, for those silenced by oppressive regimes, and for those whose silences are never heard. I also lived in a rural Georgia county with a history of racial violence and a still active Ku Klux Klan that has drawn the attention of prominent civil rights leaders, historians, and even celebrities such as Oprah. Stanford professor Patrick Phillips's recent book, Blood at the Root, *detailed the racial cleansing that led to me growing up surrounded almost exclusively by other white people. Out of this context grew a person intensely interested in how race shapes inequality in the United States. (Me!)*

As an undergraduate, I studied at a small military college in the foothills leading to the Appalachian Trail. I became obsessed with music theory. It offered a fabulous world of frequencies, which my queer and feminist self could inhabit to escape the dissonant wilderness of my surroundings. In graduate school, thanks to some really incredible feminist scholars and mentors, I discovered how these musical worlds contained cultural meanings that sonically negotiated systems of inequality. I was hooked. Thus, for my dissertation, I considered how Black and white composers used early jazz idioms after World War I—a time when the nation's racial order was anything but stable. I explored how their compositional techniques, if we listened in the right way, had much to say about racial inequality in Jim Crow America.

I currently teach at Temple University in the heart of Philadelphia, where I was hired as an assistant professor in music theory to diversify their undergraduate theory sequence—to ensure the voices silenced by the academy for hundreds of years can now be heard. (Dream job!) I'm currently writing a book to be entitled Reconstructing Whiteness: Race in the Early Jazz Marketplace, *which turns away from the high art compositions that I analyzed in my dissertation and examines instead mass industries of sound. With this new direction, I can ruminate on the relationship between money, race, and musical style. This essay, as well as my other research projects and the courses I teach at Temple, stem from my desire to figure out why so much in the rural South and the greater United States still looks and feels and sounds the same as it did one hundred years ago. In my mind, if we can figure this out, we have a brighter future. I hope you (the reader!) find the essay useful in this way too.*

Lil Nas X began his career as an unlikely internet sensation. Financially broke, he recorded a country trap song, "Old Town Road," in 2018 for fifty dollars. He promoted what he called his "country record" on TikTok for months. It did not go viral, however, until the #yeehaw challenge, where TikTok users post a video of themselves drinking "yeehaw juice" to the sound of the song's introduction and then, when the beat drops at the beginning of the first verse, magically turning into cowboys. In March, the song began to chart on the Billboard Hot 100, Hot Country Songs, and Hot R&B/Hip Hop charts. Before long, the rapper was signed to Columbia Records. In the meantime, Billboard removed "Old Town Road" from the country chart, because, according to the music institution, it failed to "embrace enough elements of today's country music to chart in its current version."[1] Lil Nas X then recorded a remix with country legend Billy Ray Cyrus. After popular backlash and a major (white) country superstar's endorsement, Billboard placed it back on the charts where it held the number one position on the Hot 100 chart for nineteen weeks, breaking a record for the longest-running number one song ever. Moreover, while his song sat at the top position, Lil Nas X publicly came out as gay on June 30, 2019, the last day of Pride Month.

Why was "Old Town Road" initially removed from the Hot Country Songs chart?[2] Many have speculated that racism and homophobia played no small part, and for good reason: country music has been criticized for its racial homogeneity and the erasure of Black roots in telling and retelling the genre's history.[3] Moreover, heteromasculinity underpins the personas of many of its most prominent cis male artists.[4] (At the time of writing, Jason Aldean's "Try That in a Small Town," with thinly veiled threats directed toward Black Lives Matter protestors, was number one on the Billboard Hot 100 Chart—the pop one, not the country one!)[5]

Yet the removal of Lil Nas X's "Old Town Road" speaks to another problem in the world of popular music—that of pigeonholing Black musicians within a certain musical style. Tethering sound to racial identity has a long history in the recording industry dating back to its inception, and an even longer history in American entertainment dating back to blackface minstrelsy of the early nineteenth century.[6] In the 1920s, recording companies and their talent scouts institutionalized preexisting views that Black musicians sounded different from white ones and argued that they should be categorized differently. Marketed as "race records," discs featuring blues, jazz, and gospel music created the only market available to Black artists.[7] Black musicians were discouraged and even prohibited from recording any other kinds of music, such as Tin Pan Alley and Broadway tunes, commercial pop music, and early forms of country called "hillbilly" or "old-time," all of which were dominated by white artists.[8]

But there were exceptions—some Black artists crossed over to white charts, usually unbeknownst to the industry, because they belied expectations of what they "should" sound like. Fletcher Henderson was one of these exceptions (Figure 1.1). A jazz bandleader, Henderson recorded a type of arranged and orchestrated jazz that was typically associated with

Figure 1.1. Fletcher Henderson, bandleader, 1926. Schomburg Center for Research in Black Culture, Photographs and Prints Division, The New York Public Library.

white bands in the early 1920s. He was a member of a growing Black middle class and received professional training. Henderson was a classically trained pianist, and he brought this musical background to his music. His arrangements featured homophonic textures, distinct and catchy melodies, and moderate syncopation, yielding a style that appealed to both Black and white jazz fans. For this reason, some of his band's recordings were not marketed as "race records" and crossed over to the (white) pop charts—a rare feat for a Black recording artist of that time.

Like Lil Nas X, Henderson defied expectations of Black musicality.[9] And yet he was still subjected to a form of industry policing that limited what kind of music he could sell. Though there are stark differences between the two musicians, especially as their careers are separated by almost a century, there are also continuities between Lil Nas X and Henderson that reveal the durability of racism in the US music industry.

In this essay, I examine how Henderson navigated the racial mechanisms of the early recording industry, while keeping Lil Nas X's experience in mind as a point of comparison. Their different experiences illuminate an ever-shifting marketplace that, at first glance, *appears* less racist today even while still adhering to much of the same anti-Black logic that underpinned its founding. My hope is that from this essay, the reader will gain insight into the economic and cultural context of our contemporary popular music landscape by studying part of its formation. To be clear, this is not a thorough account of the relationship between race and music from the 1920s to the present day but, rather, a historical exercise in which the past offers an insightful lens to view the present (and perhaps, vice versa).

HENDERSON'S STORY

The Roaring Twenties radically altered American society and culture. The Great War (1914–1918) was over, and the United States enjoyed a prominent position on the world's political stage for the first time. Economic growth, technological innovation, and increased cultural exports existed alongside rampant poverty, a rise in criminal violence, and the declining power of organized labor. This was the decade of flappers, prohibition, organized crime, the Harlem Renaissance, automobiles, consumerism, marketing, and pre-Code Hollywood. Its soundtrack was jazz. This new Black dance music dominated the ever-changing media landscape, driving the expansion of the film, radio, and record industries.[10] The biggest producer of talking machines and records, Victor Company, had only made $2.7 million in 1902. By comparison, in 1921, it earned $51 million.[11] Similarly, by 1924 Americans spent $358 million on radios and, one year later, an estimated fifty million people were tuning in.[12] These listeners preferred to listen to jazz; throughout the twenties it was what sixty to seventy percent of radio owners wanted to hear.[13]

Much of the decade's changes were racial in nature. Jim Crow segregation laws had been in effect since the 1890s, but they took on a new life in the 1920s. After World War I, Black soldiers returned home expecting equal treatment, but they were still regarded as inferior and denied the same affordances of white Americans. Black southerners continued to migrate to urban areas, shifting their predominantly white demographics. Black leaders such as W.E.B. DuBois galvanized their communities when he wrote, "We return from fighting. We return fighting."[14] The National Association for the Advancement of Colored People (NAACP) continued their anti-lynching and voting rights campaigns. Racial tension flared and culminated with the Red Summer of 1919, when mostly white-on-Black violence resulted in hundreds of deaths from twenty-five major uprisings.[15] Anti-Blackness persisted in the Jazz Age, best represented by the resurgence of the Ku Klux Klan, which by 1924 had membership numbers surpassing five million, with almost four thousand local chapters.[16]

Because of growing racial conflict in the United States, the unprecedented success of Black dance music sparked controversy among many. Many protested jazz even while its fans believed it represented the vitality and energy of the Roaring Twenties. Jazz was associated with Black working-class culture, which for many was understood to be "uncultivated" and "primitive." But it was also linked to intimate forms of dance, sex work, scantily clad women, nightclubs, illegal drinking, and interracial spaces such as black and tans (whites only clubs that featured Black entertainers). For this reason, jazz was rejected by members of both white and Black middle-class communities, though the former complained the loudest. White Americans (mis)heard the music as noisy and unrefined.[17] They believed it could disable people, atrophy brain cells, and cause insanity.[18] Much like hip hop has become, for many, a scapegoat for society's ills today, jazz was the target in the twenties for anything purportedly wrong with society, from women's short haircuts to the looming threat of socialism.[19] Religious institutions forbade it, women's temperance groups protested it, and cultural critics lambasted its deleterious effects on the moral fabric of America.[20] "We are in deadly fear of the Jazz Devil, the demon which is consuming the country," read a 1921 newspaper article.[21]

Many members of the Black middle class feared being associated with jazz for precisely these reasons, especially as they strove to prove their humanity through those cultural achievements also valued by white people. As a Black middle-class and classically trained musician, Henderson sought to ameliorate this tension in both Black and white communities and to demonstrate that Black musicians had the same skill as their white counterparts when given equal access to education and opportunities to perform and record. He created a style of jazz that appealed to middle-class listeners of all races, specifically because it drew on classical music idioms. He was well equipped to do so because of his socioeconomic background, which gave him access to musical education.

Henderson grew up in an upwardly mobile family that valued intellectualism and artistic expression. He was born and raised in Cuthbert, Georgia, which is about one hundred and forty miles south of where Lil Nas X lived in Lithia Springs. Henderson studied math and chemistry at Atlanta University (now Clark Atlanta University)—the first historically Black college or university (HBCU) in the South. Thereafter, he moved to New York to get a master's degree in chemistry at Columbia University, but his childhood musical education made the world of entertainment a place where he was more likely to have a reliable income.

Henderson's parents taught him piano beginning at age six, and he quickly developed aural and written music skills. After playing the piano with an orchestra in New York, he found work as a song plugger for one of the few Black music publishers, Pace and Handy Music Co. (named after Harry Pace and W. C. Handy).[22] In 1921, at the age of twenty-four, he became the music director of Pace's offshoot record label—Black Swan Records, the very first widely successful Black-run label. While other record companies such as Columbia and Okeh were making "race records," often steeped in offensive blackface minstrelsy imagery, Black Swan demonstrated that their music exceeded the limitations of racist stereotypes. Pace and Henderson communicated these ideals through their proximity to classical music. The label was named after Elizabeth Taylor Greenfield, who was a well-known Black concert singer of the mid-nineteenth century.[23] They also had an art music series which drew financial backing from the NAACP. Members of what Du Bois called the "Talented Tenth," Black Swan's employees and musicians leveraged their talent to forge new opportunities that had only previously been assigned to white Americans.

Though the record label was a rare example of success in a white-dominated industry (and notably folded a few years later for this very reason), there was a growing force of middle-class Black musicians whose classical training influenced their experimental approaches to popular music—Henderson among them.[24] After touring with the Black Swan Troubadours to provide piano accompaniment for famous blues singers such as Ethel Waters, Henderson put his own dance orchestra together.[25] In the first eighteen months of its existence, they produced hundreds of records—on par only with the leading white bands.[26] Though the bulk of their work together happened in live performances, the orchestra's recorded output indexed Henderson's prowess in the marketplace. He was deftly attuned to the ways in which Black music was becoming more popular and how Black musicians forged increased opportunities to challenge racist stereotypes. He exploited these racial changes in a way that benefited his musical career and those of his orchestra members.

In the mid-1920s, he started working with arranger Don Redman—another important business move for his ensemble. Redman was also a Black middle-class Southern musician who sought formal training and developed skills as a composer and multi-instrumentalist. In his arrangements, Redman's melodies were always clear and catchy, his syncopated rhythms smooth. But he also preferred complex textural contrast to maintain an energetic drive and bring peak entertainment quality to any three-minute song. His approach to arranging dance orchestra music helped usher in the swing era. In particular, he used small combinations of instruments to create different sections (brass and reeds, for example) that interacted with call and response—exactly what you might hear in one of the most well-known big band songs today, Benny Goodman's "Sing, Sing, Sing" (1937).[27] In the 1930s, he composed for many of the greatest swing orchestras including Count Basie and Jimmy Dorsey. With Redman at the helm, Henderson's group became well-known for their intricate arrangements and signature dance orchestra sound, which American music scholar Jeffrey Magee describes as "a unique, savvy synthesis of contemporary urban popular music, classical gestures, and blues, ragtime, and jazz."[28]

Audio Example 1.1. "Sugar Foot Stomp," Fletcher Henderson's Orchestra, May 29, 1925, Columbia 395-D. https://doi.org/10.3998/mpub.13006960.cmp.2[29]

"Sugar Foot Stomp" is often cited as one of Henderson's best recordings, because it captures his quintessential aesthetic.[30] It is based on "Dipper Mouth Blues," written and recorded by King Oliver and Louis Armstrong in 1923.[31] Armstrong, during his short stint with Henderson in New York, asked Redman to arrange one of the melodies Armstrong had written with Oliver, while playing in his band in Chicago. Redman used his expertise with contrast to transform a densely textured series of improvisational sections into a tapestry of rich interactions among instruments. In the original "Dipper Mouth Blues," the trumpet, clarinet, and trombone improvised at the same time—known as collective or polyphonic improvisation—which produced a chorus of competing, interwoven melodies and rhythmic patterns. In "Sugar Foot Stomp," however, the melody is prioritized while small sections of instruments, always in dialogue with one another, create harmonic support and a homophonic texture. Redman consistently changes the texture for endless variety—a prized possession of any early jazz hit—to intrigue listeners and dancers with novelty. The song also features contrasting timbres as the instruments switch up for each formal section (Table 1.1). For compositional

Table 1.1. Analysis of "Sugar Foot Stomp," Fletcher Henderson's Orchestra, May 29, 1925, Columbia 395-D.[75]

Time	Section	Measures	Description
0:00	Intro	4 mm	Ensemble alternates with trumpets rapidly descending in harmonized thirds
0:04	A	12 mm	Alto saxophone solos main melody with repeated rhythmic figure while ensemble accentuates backbeat; last two measures feature break with all saxophones
0:18	A	12 mm	Brass repeat with some sparse collective improvisation
0:32	B	16 mm (8 + 8)	Clarinet trio, harmonizing, introduce new melody and straighter rhythmic patterns over the ensemble's backbeats; one-measure ensemble interjections in the last measure of each phrase with a common ragtime rhythm
0:51	C	12 mm	Trombone solo reanimates the rhythm by quoting the A melody while the banjo plays accented accompaniment; the rhythm section featuring tuba, banjo, and drums creates a backbeat; last two measures feature break with all saxophones
1:05	D	12 mm	Trumpet solo begins with long repeated notes and varies melody to delineate the three phrases of the 12-bar blues form over the rhythm section; ensemble returns in last two measures
1:19	D	12 mm	Trumpet solo begins with stop-time and then continues to solo over the rhythm section's strong backbeats; ensemble returns in last two measures again

Time	Section	Measures	Description
1:33	D	12 mm	Trumpet solo creates variation with a long note high in its register over the rhythm section; stop-time textures break up repetition in this third cycle of D; ends with vocal break, "Oh, play that thing!"
1:48	E	12 mm	Entire ensemble creates contrast with quietly played and smooth, legato lines in a dirge-like manner, tight-knit harmonies, and a more complex harmonic progression; they introduce new melodic ideas but return to the spiky syncopated rhythms in the last phrase; concludes with single-note clarinet break
2:02	A	12 mm	Ensemble repeats A section but with dense collective improvisation, a web of cross-rhythms, and a four-beat lightly swinging rhythm section; last two measures comprise stop-time cadence
2:17	E	12 mm	Repeats above E section
2:31	A	12 mm	Repeats above A section; trumpet-dominated stop-time cadence
2:44	Coda	2 mm	Quiet saxophone tag with smooth voice leading

variation, Redman also uses breaks (when the rhythm section and ensemble stop playing while a soloists or small group of instruments briefly continue) and tags (adding a few extra measures of music at the end of a complete phrase). The song was one of "the best-selling records of late 1925." It was recorded many times and "became the model on which other bands based their versions into the 1940s."[32]

With such hits as "Sugar Foot Stomp," Henderson's band secured a residential position at one of the most prestigious ballrooms in downtown Manhattan—the Roseland Ballroom (Figure 1.2). Although not as elite and well-paying as hotel ballrooms, which hired mostly white bands, the Roseland was well-known for its spaciousness, elevated stage, and sophisticated architectural design—with ornately painted walls, large columns, and a vaulted ceiling. The Roseland featured both Black and white ensembles, although by law they had to perform at different times. The ballroom mostly catered to young white people interested in dancing in a more "refined" manner.[33] In this urbane space, Henderson's orchestra wore tuxedos, performed complicated arrangements, and read from sheet

Figure 1.2. The interior of the Roseland Ballroom, 1920s. Mary Evans Picture Library, Media Storehouse, Ltd.

music with adept literacy—all class signifiers that betrayed stereotypes about Black musicians as uneducated and unrefined. With Henderson's weekly engagement at the Roseland and steady flow of recordings, the classically trained musicians of his orchestra made Black dance music accessible to a broad audience in the 1920s.

NAVIGATING THE EARLY RECORDING INDUSTRY

Henderson's orchestra chronicled new territory for Black musicians within a white-dominated industry that set protocols for marketing Black music. In this section, I describe this economy and consider how Henderson's musical career and style, like that of Lil Nas X's, was constricted by racial stereotypes. Three marketplace parameters especially limited Black creative expression as well as financial gain. These are: 1) record labels recording all Black music, regardless of its genre or style, on "race records"; 2) the use of marketing terms for different types of jazz that reinforced false conceptions of race as biological; and 3) inequitable access and opportunity. All of these parameters were both informed by and reinforced ideas about how Black culture *should* sound and what type of music Black Americans *should* play.

Race Records

As I mentioned in the introduction, the 1920s marked a distinct turning point for Black music. Though such blues and ragtime musicians as Wilbur Sweatman and James Reese Europe recorded prior to this time, Black music was being promoted in profoundly different ways.[34] Industry men (recording label owners, talent scouts, and managers, for example), who were primarily white, peddled what were called "race records" with a distinct audience in mind. Many cite the unprecedented success of Mamie Smith's "Crazy Blues" (1920) as the recording that ignited this paradigm shift.[35] Black composer Perry Bradford wrote the song and pushed Okeh records to hire Smith to record it; but her previous two recordings with the company ("That Thing Called Love" and "You Can't Keep a Good

Man Down") were not very successful, so they hired the white Sophie Tucker instead. However, in an incredible twist of fate, Tucker could not, in the end, make the recording date and at the last minute the label executives hired Smith to record Bradford's new hit, "Crazy Blues."[36] Smith's recording reportedly sold seventy-five thousand copies in Harlem and more in Chicago and Philadelphia—all Black epicenters of creativity—in just a short amount of time. White industry men began to realize the potential of marketing Black music to Black listeners, not just white ones. Thereafter, Black musicians began to occupy a more significant portion of the market and, as such, gained more control over representations of their own culture.

The race record category, according to historian Karl Hagstrom Miller, functioned both as an advertisement and a form of censorship.[37] Race records were marketed in opposition to old-time (or hillbilly) records, which circumscribed a working-class Southern oral tradition played by string bands and fiddlers. Though both Black and white musicians were versed in this music, only white Southerners were recorded with this designation. Anything Black people made—from sermons and vaudeville skits to blues, jazz, and concert music—was placed in the race records category. (Positioned in opposition was Tin Pan Alley and other mass-produced pop songs—which featured only white and mostly Northern, urban musicians.) Miller argues that with these categories the industry was forcibly "segregating sound." For Black musicians, who played a variety of styles including mass-produced pop tunes, "the label 'race record' did not identify a musical sound or style," writes Miller. "It defined the race of a musician."[38]

These style and genre distinctions failed to capture what was really happening in the daily lives of musicians of all races, because they falsely indicated a biological relationship between musical style and racial identity.[39] While the industry was very much at play in establishing this problematic relationship, consumers reinforced these ideological links with their listening habits. Jennifer Lynn Stoever, Erich Nunn, and Nina Eidsheim all write about the racial bias baked into listening practices.[40]

Eidsheim, in her research on vocal timbre, demonstrates how listeners believe they can identify a person based on a singer's tone. Because the voice is located inside of the person, is part of the person, the human voice is understood to be a "cue to interiority, essence, and unmediated identity"—that is, not just *who the singer is* but *what kind of person they are*. Such an assumption has grave consequences in a society structured by racial hierarchies, where listeners, as Nunn writes, "experience music as possessing, producing, or reinforcing racial attributes."[41] In this way, the ear is not a neutral part of the body, simply playing its part in the five senses, but rather a subjective part of the body drawing on cultural ideas to interpret the meanings of sound. As Stoever puts it, the ear is an "organ of racial discernment."[42] In the 1920s, audiences operated under these conditions, believing that there were radical distinctions between "Black" and "white" music. To sell records, then, white industry men policed what Jennifer Lynn Stoever calls a "sonic color line."[43]

Henderson had to negotiate this vicious cycle of industry expectations and consumer practices. And, at times, he challenged the sonic color line. Some of his recordings were not automatically placed under the "race records" designation. Instead, they crossed over to the mainstream (white) pop chart, because their sophisticated approach to arranged dance music was more frequently associated with white jazz bands. White bandleaders such as Jean Goldkette and Paul Whiteman formulated a strain of Black dance music that was wrapped in classical music's visual and aural symbols while still signaling jazz to its primarily white listenership. Concert stage settings, tuxedos, printed sheet music, and music stands were coupled with orchestrated dance tunes to make jazz more palatable to middle-class and white audiences. Henderson's orchestra did the same, proving that Black musicians were highly educated and professional and that this style of jazz did not belong exclusively to white men. Even though Henderson challenged the sonic color line at times, he was also confined by it. For example, his orchestra played dance arrangements of classical repertoire such as waltzes.[44] They never recorded these, however, likely because recording companies assumed it would not sell.

Different Jazz Styles on Race Records

In many of his recordings, Henderson arranged a different style of jazz than was typically associated with Black musicians. Not all jazz was the same, and in Jim Crow America those stylistic differences had racialized meaning. The industry used the word "hot" to market many Black jazz records in an effort to signify a distinction from their white counterparts. The term signaled to audiences that the style of music performed might be more syncopated, improvised, polyphonic, and played by smaller ensembles. Whiteman's and Henderson's music, on the other hand, was more fully orchestrated, arranged, and rehearsed. It also featured clear melodies, homophonic textures, and less improvisation and syncopation. The label "hot" circulated widely and had cultural currency among listeners, dancers, musicians, booking agents, record labels, A&R men, music publishers, and venue managers. Song titles and band names abounded with this overdetermined word, and Victor Records even had a hot jazz series in the latter half of the 1920s. Some Black musicians, such as Jelly Roll Morton and Louis Armstrong, marshaled this term as a pathway to success within a limiting framework for marketing their music. But it's important to note that Jelly Roll Morton with his Red Hot Peppers, and Louis Armstrong and His Hot Seven's recording, "Hotter Than That," also captured a tradition they valued. It was more than a marketing label. White groups began to exploit this word and its attendant style, especially as jazz became less controversial and more popular among white, collegiate youth who sought out "hot" bands.[45] The term, then, was used purposefully to market what Eidsheim calls "sonic Blackness" and not necessarily the musicians' racial identities.[46]

Linking the word "hot" to certain musical elements drew on problematic stereotypes about so-called Black "primitivity." During the rise of Jim Crow segregation in the 1890s, aural perceptions of Black music changed. It became associated exclusively with rhythm.[47] A departure from the luscious harmonies of the spirituals during Reconstruction, ragtime, jazz, and blues were constituted only by an ecstatic pulse, syncopation, and erratic dance moves. White Euro-American music, on the other hand, was perceived to be more about harmonic and melodic complexity and therefore *the opposite of* rhythmically driven Black music. Yet jazz and its precursors were as much about texture, timbre, innovative pitch collections, and harmonic ingenuity as they were about rhythm. Simplifying a rich tradition down to this single characteristic facilitated the link between Black American culture and African primitivity, animated by white imaginations of African drumming. If Black music was "willfully misunderstood" as primitive, because it was perceived to be unchanging since the inception of the Atlantic slave trade, then "hot rhythm signified the antithesis of civilized artistic practice."[48]

While the term "hot" constructed a binary between white and Black jazz, Henderson's orchestra challenged this racial signifier. For example, their performance venue, the Roseland, did not advertise the band's music as jazz but rather "high-grade" orchestral dance music.[49] Their sound aligned with the cultivated traditions of elite musicianship. They challenged the mapping of "hot" jazz onto Black skin, and they separated orchestrated jazz and whiteness, especially as they performed elaborate arrangements effortlessly. Henderson's orchestra also challenged this binary by recording both "hotter" tunes alongside Tin Pan Alley songs and Broadway tunes. With titles such as "Red Hot Mama," "Just Hot," "Oh! Sister, Ain't That Hot," and with some of their "hotter" players, such as saxophonist Coleman Hawkins and trumpeter Howard Scott, the band demonstrated their professional versatility as men acutely aware of the mosaic of styles their audiences enjoyed hearing.

Challenging racial stereotypes had a social impact that exceeded the musical practice of recording "race records." The stakes were much higher because ideas about culture and sound were used as "evidence" in theories of racial difference and inferiority. Pseudosciences like phrenology and eugenics proliferated in the United States at the turn of the twentieth century. Seeking to "improve" the (white) human race, eugenicists espoused violent tactics such as sterilization and strict segregation. After World War I, there was a resurgence of these ideas; Lothrop Stoddard's *The Rising Tide of Color against White World-Supremacy* (1920), Earnest Cox's *White*

America (1922), and numerous reissues of Madison Grant's 1916 text, *The Passing of the Great Race*, topped bookshelves and advocated for eugenical solutions to "preserve the racial integrity" of the white race.[50] By the late 1920s, nearly four hundred college eugenics courses existed.[51] In many of the texts that students might have studied, Black music was "proof" of racial inferiority—in part because of how white people (mis)heard and reconstituted this music as simplistic and rhythmic.[52] In fact, entire theories of music have emerged from this logic, demonstrating that the ear really was "an organ of racial discernment."[53] White aural imagining of Black musical practices supported segregationist logic. Music became just as important as legislation in expressing the (il)logic of US racial hierarchies. To work against these stereotypes, then, was to fight not just for the right to record what you wanted but also for the right to live.

Access and Opportunity

Despite his success, Henderson still experienced disparities in access, profits, and opportunities compared to white bandleaders. In general, Black bands had to travel more to earn a living. White bands, on the other hand, had illustrious long-term contracts with more prestigious (and higher-paying) venues. Traveling while Black was dangerous, especially in the South, as one could be subjected to vigilante violence and harassment at any given moment. This lifestyle took a toll on a musician's personal health and family life. Black bands also received far less money for their songs, live performances, and recordings. They were less likely to have long-term recording contracts with a single major label and more likely to record frequently across a variety of labels to earn a living. Black musicians were often paid a small fee for a single recording session instead of accumulating royalties from copyrights or mechanical reproductions. White bandleaders, such as Jean Goldkette, Roger Wolfe Kahn, Vincent Lopez, and Paul Whiteman, fared much better in the marketplace because of their racial privilege.

Whiteman serves as an interesting point of comparison to Henderson in this regard. He was the largest profiteer of Black music, and yet he played a similar style of jazz to Henderson. He was more successful and high-profile than any other musician in the 1920s associated with the word "jazz." In advertisements and promotional materials, he was billed as its king. His first hit, "Whispering" (1920), sold so many copies it helped financially support the company that recorded it, Victor Talking Machine Company, the leading competitor in the market by 1923.[54] As an introduction into the world of jazz, it was quite mild and erred on the conservative side compared to some of his later recordings. A series of choruses guide the listener through changing solo instruments which play the song's catchy melody while the rest of the orchestra (strings included) quietly supports. A bit of syncopation in the first few cycles takes on more rhythmic nuance toward the end in a bid to gesture toward improvisation. This was just enough to whet the sonic appetites of his growing audience.

In 1924, Whiteman debuted George Gershwin's *Rhapsody in Blue* at Aeolian Hall in New York, explicating jazz's artistic ability. It was so well received that Whiteman's orchestra went on several national and international tours with the hit, and numerous recordings and sheet music printings of *Rhapsody* sold in the millions. As jazz became less controversial—in no small part because of the work of Whiteman and Henderson—Whiteman began to experiment with more complicated arrangements featuring increased syncopation and improvisation. "Changes" (1926) and "San" (1928) are two such examples. Both songs featured skilled players Bix Beiderbecke (trumpet), Frankie Trumbauer (trombone), Tommy Dorsey (trombone), and Jimmy Dorsey (alto saxophone).[55] While "Changes" has an impressive Beiderbecke solo and some scatting by Bing Crosby, "San" draws on the techniques that appear in Henderson's "Sugar Foot Stomp," recorded two years prior. It is highly likely that Whiteman's arranger, Bill Challis, had the increasingly well-known Redman arrangements in mind.[56]

Whiteman's ability to satisfy the changing tastes of his largely (though not exclusively) white audience, along with his racial privilege, led to extreme financial gain.[57] By 1924, Paul Whiteman Inc. laid claim to fifty-two satellite orchestras with locations both in and beyond the

United States, including Paris, Havana, London, and Mexico.[58] In 1925, he made more money than he ever would again: $800,000—the equivalent of roughly $14 million today.[59] Much of this came from touring *Rhapsody in Blue*. A household name, he was offered deals with many advertisers, marketing products from automobiles to milk. While Black musicians were searching for single recording sessions, Whiteman had lengthy contracts with large, financially stable labels. After eight years with Victor, he switched to Columbia in 1928 simply because they offered him more money. To secure the biggest name in entertainment history up to that date, Columbia tripled his annual salary to $75,000 (worth over $1.3 million today). Moreover he was given amenities that almost no other artists received, namely a percentage of company profits, additional royalties on his recordings, and a seat on the board of directors.[60] By the close of the decade, he hosted a weekly radio show, which paid him $5,000 for each one-hour broadcast, and he inspired and starred in his very own feature film, *King of Jazz*.[61] Whether a white man deserved the appellation or not, he had become the music's king, not Henderson or any other Black American.

Within this industry context, Henderson still managed to do things that no other Black bandleader could. He set records for the number of arrangements his band recorded, his music crossed over to the white pop charts, and he secured permanent positions at upscale venues. The Roseland also had nightly radio broadcasts on a small network that became famous for advertising the latest entertainment in nightclubs and cabarets across the color line, even while larger networks stuck to prestigious venues featuring only white bands.[62] These broadcasts continued into the 1930s when he started performing at Connie's Inn, and his arrangements for white bands, such as Benny Goodman's, showed up on larger network stations in the mid-1930s.[63] Though his musical activity decreased in the 1940s, he witnessed before his death in 1952 the transformation of jazz into "America's classical music" with the advent of bebop. For someone who championed the artistic value of Black popular music for much of his life, this must have been satisfying.

THE UNCROWNED KING OF JAZZ

Much like Lil Nas X, Henderson challenged society's musical-racial ideas by successfully making music largely perceived to be "white." This perception was misguided, and it erased decades of Black ingenuity. The artistic cultivation of Black folk and popular music dated back to the nineteenth century with, for example, the compositions of Samuel Coleridge-Taylor and Harry T. Burleigh. Likewise, Lil Nas X highlighted the Black roots of country music, joining conversations by artists like award-winning banjoist Rhiannon Giddens (of the Carolina Chocolate Drops). Henderson's and Lil Nas X's challenges to dominant racial stereotypes did not come without consequences. Whereas Lil Nas X was subjected to industry policing at the start of his career, Henderson's music was policed after the height of his career in jazz histories documenting the 1920s and early 1930s. In this section, I explore how some of the historical treatment of Henderson reflects past and present gatekeeping within jazz.

In *The Uncrowned King of Swing: Fletcher Henderson and Big Band Jazz*, Jeffrey Magee demonstrates Henderson's formidable influence on early and big band jazz with detailed analysis of his recordings. His book's title draws attention to Henderson's work as an arranger for the white Benny Goodman who, like Paul Whiteman, was dubbed king of a genre and built his success on decades of Black creative labor. But the title also speaks to the way in which Henderson's legacy has been handled in jazz discourse.[64] Henderson's life and music are not without scholarly representation, but the parameters by which his contributions to jazz are measured come with a host of value judgments designed to validate some jazz styles over others.[65]

In early jazz histories, Henderson is often overshadowed by Louis Armstrong, who played in the Henderson orchestra for a short time and went on to become one of America's most treasured musicians. Armstrong is hailed for his "hot" jazz and for pioneering improvisational soloing. This great-man narrative permeates old and new accounts of the music. In one of the first histories of early jazz written in 1968, author Gunther Schuller dedicates an entire chapter to Armstrong who is dubbed "The First Great Soloist." By comparison, Henderson's orchestra is folded into a larger chapter on New York dance bands. Schuller also paints Henderson as an unsavvy professional who lacked the "tenacious drive" of Armstrong and achieved success because he happened to be in the right place at the right time.[66] Today's leading jazz history textbook, *Jazz*, maintains this imbalance by introducing the New Orleans trumpeter in a chapter entitled: "Louis Armstrong and the First Great Soloists."[67] No doubt Armstrong merits this attention, but Henderson had extensively more fame and success in the 1920s than Armstrong. What does this rhetorical strategy say about how we define jazz and circumscribe the legitimacy of its musicians? I think it siloes both arranging and commercialism, while prizing solo improvisation.

Valuing solo improvisation over arranging has a long history in jazz discourse. Such canonical figures as Charlie Parker, Miles Davis, John Coltrane, and Duke Ellington are praised for their "original" compositions and extemporaneously "inspired" performances. Music that is rehearsed, polished, and designed to entertain mass audiences is diminished in these historical accounts in order to construct jazz as individualistic, virtuosic, always extemporaneous, and never commercial.[68] Armstrong as "the first great soloist" buttresses this narrative in a way that Henderson's music does not. But in the 1920s, arranging had serious cultural import in making good jazz because audiences wanted to dance, not listen intently to extended solos. Magee's scholarship serves as an important corrective in this regard, reminding us that early jazz was dance music and Henderson made people dance.

Music in the service of entertainment and dancing is often scrutinized by those who believe commercial success tarnishes the artistic and intellectual brilliance of jazz. Magee shows how this value judgment was used to delegitimize Henderson and understate his impact. He directs us to one of the first examples of jazz criticism. In *The Real Jazz*, published in 1942, French author Hugues Panassié ridiculed Henderson for his "commercial concessions" and his attempt to be the "Paul Whiteman of the race."[69] Panassié goes on to establish a distinction between false and true jazz, in which Henderson falls into the former category precisely because of his success in the marketplace and his relationship to written-out arrangements. Disdain for commercialism persists well into the twenty-first century, especially as jazz discourse has clung to romanticized stories of financially suffering artists. Within this mythology, musicians would rather choose starvation than succumb to the market, which might compromise their artistic integrity. In the 1920s, Armstrong adheres to this formulaic mold of "authentic" jazz musicianship more easily than Henderson for two reasons: 1) he struggled to find success (at least initially); and 2) unlike Henderson, he grew up in poverty, playing music on the street to survive. This thinking has grave implications though. As one of the leading jazz scholars Scott DeVeaux writes, trying to keep jazz separate from the marketplace "[demonizes] the economic system that allows musicians to survive—and from this demon there is no escape."[70]

While the gatekeeping I describe above does not compare to being relegated to race records or a certain style of music during a musician's lifetime, or to being ripped off the country charts for simply being Black (as was the case with Lil Nas X), it does demonstrate the different ways that Black musicians are policed and judged when they belie white expectations of Black musicality. For some musicians this means being erased from historical narratives, for others it means being deprived of the financial gain to which they are entitled. In this regard, Lil Nas X has fared better than Henderson in the twenty-first century. After a social media backlash, "Old Town Road" was placed back onto the charts and the artist was offered a lucrative recording contract with Columbia Records. Two years later, he released his debut full-length album *Montero*, which garnered widespread acclaim; "Montero (Call Me by Your Name)" and "Industry Baby" received Grammy nominations.[71] Further, his achievements reignited conversations about country music's Black origins and paved the way for continued and new contributions, evidenced most notably in Beyoncé's recent country album, *Cowboy Carter* (2024). Over one hundred years ago, only white musicians recording Black music could achieve the economic success and have the cultural impact of someone like Lil Nas X.

CONCLUSION

Though Henderson's and Lil Nas X's experiences are quite different, there is something to be gained by putting them in dialogue with each other, especially as it speaks to the racial inheritances of our past. Black intellectuals have long argued that much of the infrastructure of the Atlantic slave trade persists well into the twenty-first century. Angela Davis and Michelle Alexander, for example, point out that state institutions and policies facilitate a form of mass incarceration that mirrors the anti-Black subjugation of slavery and Jim Crow segregation. For this reason, Alexander dubs our current racial order the New Jim Crow.[72] Though the "old" Jim Crow legally ended with landmark legislation such as *Brown vs. Board of Education* in 1954, which sought to promote the integration of schools, and the Civil Rights Act of 1964, which prohibited any form of discrimination, Alexander persuasively argues that the race-based policies of our incarceration system recycle previous approaches to maintaining inequality. If the juridical, cultural, and social principles of older racial orders are still with us, what bearing does this have on US music?

Though much has changed since the 1920s, there are consistent features that unveil the racial apparatus at the heart of the music industry. The issue of "kings" is but one example and has emerged several times in this essay already. Whiteman was the "King of Jazz," Goodman was the "King of Swing," Elvis Presley was the "King of Rock'n'Roll," and Eminem was crowned the "King of Hip-Hop" by *Rolling Stone* in 2011.[73] Put differently, the music industry still rewards—whether in titular or monetary form—white interpreters of Black music more than Black musicians.

At the same time, the music industry also continues to gatekeep Black musicians who challenge stylistic boundaries. Lil Nas X is not alone. In 2020, Tyler, the Creator won a Grammy for the genre-defying album *Igor.* And although the album's tracks pay respect to funk, R&B, and neo soul, the Recording Academy placed it in the Best Rap Album category, presumably because the artist is Black. Tyler, the Creator was outraged. So too were his fans. In an interview, he trenchantly describes the industry's racism: "it sucks that whenever we, and I mean guys that look like me, do anything that's genre-bending, they always put it in a 'rap' or 'urban' category. I don't like that 'urban' word. To me, it's just a politically correct way to say the N-word," he said.[74] Or perhaps a politically correct way to say "race record."

Fletcher Henderson's story challenges us to think critically about not only the racist mechanisms of the marketplace that restrict Black musicians *during* their career but also how they will be included in the stories we tell about American music history thereafter. With this in mind, our challenge in analyzing Lil Nas X's music career is different, given his unprecedented success today and his ability to push back against industry racism. The question that remains, then, is: how will his radical genre-defying music be remembered in our history textbooks?

NOTES

1. Elias Leight, "Lil Nas X's 'Old Town Road' Was a Country Hit. Then Country changed Its Mind," *Rolling Stone*, March 26, 2019, https://www.rollingstone.com/music/music-features/lil-nas-x-old-town-road-810844/.
2. For the song, see Lil Nas X, "Old Town Road (Official Video) ft. Billy Ray Cyrus," music video, YouTube, July 19, 2019, https://www.youtube.com/watch?v=r7qovpFAGrQ.
3. For more on this topic, see: Diane Pecknold, ed., *Hidden in the Mix: The African American Presence in Country Music* (Duke University Press, 2013); Francesca T. Royster, *Black Country Music: Listening for Revolutions* (University of Texas Press, 2022).
4. For more on this topic, see: Shana Goldin-Perschbacher, *Queer Country* (University of Illinois Press, 2022); Kristine M. McCusker and Diane Pecknold, eds., *A Boy Named Sue: Gender and Country Music* (University Press of Mississippi, 2004).
5. For an explanation of the complicated reasons this song topped the charts, see: Chris Molanphy, "How Jason Aldean Rode Liberal Outrage to the Top of the Hot 100: Why a "Canceled" Song is Atop the Pop Charts—and Country Singers Hold the Top 3 for the First Time Ever," Slate, August 3, 2023, https://slate.com/culture/2023/08/jason-aldean-try-that-in-a-small-town-billboard-country.html.
6. Though recorded music circulated well before the 1920s, it was not until after World War I that recordings began to supplant sheet music as the primary medium consumers purchased, thus marking the beginning of a new

industry. For more on blackface minstrelsy, see: Dale Cockrell, *Demons of Disorder: Early Blackface Minstrels and their World* (Cambridge University Press, 1997).

7. Karl Hagstrom Miller, *Segregating Sound: Inventing Folk and Pop Music in the Age of Jim Crow* (Duke University Press, 2010), 187–214.
8. Elijah Wald, *Escaping the Delta: Robert Johnson and the Invention of the Blues* (Amistad Press, 2004), 52, 61–62, and 97; Hagstrom Miller, *Segregating Sound*, 215—241.
9. In this essay, I write extensively about Fletcher Henderson as representative of Black innovation in the 1920s. His career and success, however, were dependent on his close collaborations with others, including his orchestra members, arrangers, and connections within Black entertainment circles, especially in Manhattan. For the sake of clarity, however, I will often reference Henderson alone while keeping in mind the collective of artists he worked with that made his success possible.
10. See: Burton W. Peretti, *The Creation of Jazz: Music, Race, and Culture in Urban America* (University of Illinois Press, 1992); Elijah Wald, *How the Beatles Destroyed Rock'n'Roll* (Oxford University Press, 2009); Kathy J. Ogren, *The Jazz Revolution: Twenties America and the Meaning of Jazz* (Oxford University Press, 1989).
11. Ogren, *Jazz Revolution*, 152.
12. Susan Douglas, *Listening In: Radio and the American Imagination* (Random House, 1999), 52; Wald, *How the Beatles*, 92.
13. Wald, *How the Beatles*, 92; Ogren, *Jazz Revolution*, 154.
14. W. E. B. DuBois, "Returning Soldiers," *The Crisis* 18, no. 1 (May 1919), 14.
15. Cameron McWhirter, *Red Summer: The Summer of 1919 and the Awakening of Black America* (St. Martin's Griffin, 2011), 15.
16. Nancy K. MacLean, *Behind the Mask of Chivalry: The Making of the Second Ku Klux Klan* (Oxford University Press, 1994), 10.
17. Karl Koenig, ed., *Jazz in Print (1856–1929): An Anthology of Selected Early Readings in Jazz History* (Pendragon Press, 2002), 75, 134–136, 145, 194, 241, 243, 244, 257, 278, 285, 315, 319, 326, 358, 408, 419, 442, 467, 484, 505, 524, and 536.
18. Russell L. Johnson, "'Disease is Unrhythmical': Jazz, Health, and Disability in 1920s America," *Health and History* 13, no. 2 (2011): 17–18.
19. See the following primary source for an example of scapegoating jazz: R. W. S. Mendl, *The Appeal of Jazz* (Philip Allan, 1927), 186–187. For more on critiques of hip hop, see: Tricia Rose, *The Hip Hop Wars: What We Talk About When We Talk About Hip Hop—and Why It Matters* (Basic Books, 2008).
20. Koenig, *Jazz in Print*, 171, 214, 227, 235, and 238.

21. Carrie Allen Tipton, "Who's Afraid of the Jazz Monsters? For many Americans, jazz was the music of demons, devils, and things that go bump in the night," *History Today* 69, no. 10 (October 2019), https://www.historytoday.com/history-matters/whos-afraid-jazz-monsters. Also see: Ogren, *Jazz Revolution*, 140–161.
22. For a fascinating history of Harry Pace and Black Swan Records, see "The Vanishing of Harry Pace," WNYC Studios, June 2021, https://www.wnycstudios.org/series/vanishing-harry-pace.
23. For more on Greenfield, see: Julia Chybowski, "Jenny Lind and the Making of Mainstream American Popular Music," in *Open Access Musicology, Volume 1*, ed. Daniel Barolsky and Louis Epstein (Lever Press, 2020), https://www.fulcrum.org/epubs/j098zd015/OEBPS/OAM-0011.xhtml#ch07.
24. Other examples include James P. Johnson, Edmund Thornton Jenkins, Will Marion Cook, William Grant Still, and Duke Ellington, among others. I highly recommend John Howland's book on this topic: *Ellington Uptown: Duke Ellington, James P. Johnson, and the Birth of Concert Jazz* (University of Michigan Press, 2009). Also see my article about Jenkins and Still: Stephanie Doktor, "Finding Florence Mills: The Voice of the Harlem Jazz Queen in the Compositions of William Grant Still and Edmund Thornton Jenkins," *Journal of the Society for American Music* 14, no. 4 (November 2020): 451–479. For more on Black classical music, see: Kira Thurman, *Singing Like Germans: Black Musicians in the Land of Bach, Beethoven, and Brahms* (Cornell University Press, 2021); and Samantha Ege and Douglas Shadle, "As Her Music Is Reconsidered, a Composer Turns 135. Again." *New York Times*, April 7, 2023, https://www.nytimes.com/2023/04/07/arts/music/florence-price-music.html.
25. All of the biographical facts in this paragraph come from the only up-to-date and thorough scholarly treatment of Henderson and his music, to which I return later in the essay: Jeffrey Magee, *The Uncrowned King of Swing: Fletcher Henderson and Big Band Jazz* (Oxford University Press, 2005), 16–26. Also see: Walter C. Allen, *Hendersonia: The Music of Fletcher Henderson and His Musicians: A Bio-Discography* (Walter C. Allen [self-published], 1973).
26. Magee, *Uncrowned King*, 34.
27. For the song, see Benny Goodman, "Sing, Sing, Sing," YouTube, (1939?), https://www.youtube.com/watch?v=r2S1I_ien6A.
28. Magee, *Uncrowned King*, 5–6.
29. Time stamps may differ slightly depending on the recording speed and streaming media.
30. For the song, see Fletcher Henderson, "Sugar Foot Stomp – New York City, May 29, 1925," YouTube, https://www.youtube.com/watch?v=15BDLxRc05Y.

31. For the song, see King Oliver Jazz Band, "Dipper Mouth Blues," YouTube, June 23, 1923, https://www.youtube.com/watch?v=ueAcG23HL08.
32. Magee, *Uncrowned King*, 89.
33. Magee, *Uncrowned King*, 35.
34. See the following for the impact of James Reese Europe on these market developments: David Gilbert, *The Product of Our Souls: Ragtime, Race, and the Birth of the Manhattan Musical Marketplace* (University of North Carolina Press, 2015).
35. Hagstrom Miller, *Segregating Sound*, 189–194; Allan Sutton, *Race Records and the American Recording Industry, 1919–1945* (Mainspring Press, 2016), 9–20. To listen to "Crazy Blues," see Mamie Smith, "Crazy Blues," YouTube, August 10, 1920, https://www.youtube.com/watch?v=qaz4Ziw_CfQ.
36. Hagstrom Miller, *Segregating Sound*, 190–191.
37. Hagstrom Miller, *Segregating Sound*, 188.
38. Hagstrom Miller, *Segregating Sound*, 220.
39. Hagstrom Miller gives innumerable examples of this cross-pollination in his seventh chapter, "Black Folk and Hillbilly Pop," 215–240.
40. Nina Eidsheim, *The Race of Sound: Listening, Timbre, and Vocality in African American Music* (Duke University Press, 2018); Erich Nunn, *Sounding the Color Line: Music and Race in the Southern Imagination* (University of Georgia Press, 2015); Jennifer Lynn Stoever, *The Sonic Color Line: Race and the Cultural Politics of Listening* (New York University Press, 2016).
41. Eidsheim, *Race of Sound*, 67; Nunn, *Sounding the Color Line*, 5.
42. Stoever, *Sonic Color Line*, 4.
43. Stoever, *Sonic Color Line*, 1–9. In coining this phrase, Stoever is drawing on Black intellectual and political leader W. E. B. Du Bois, who wrote in 1903 that "the problem of the twentieth century is the problem of the color line." W. E. B. Du Bois, *The Souls of Black Folk: Essays and Sketches*, 8th ed. (A. C. McClurg & Co., 1909), vii and 13.
44. Magee, *Uncrowned King*, 7–8.
45. The California Ramblers, Ted Lewis, and Jean Goldkette began to record arrangements based on dense textures, improvisation, syncopation, and expressive solos. Red Nichols, known for his "hot" jazz, sold one million copies of "Ida, Sweet as Apple Cider" in 1927. See: Joseph Murrells, *The Book of Golden Discs*, 2nd ed., (Barrie and Jenkins, 1978), 16.
46. Eidsheim, *Race of Sound*, 61–90.
47. Ronald Radano, "Hot Fantasies: American Modernism and the Idea of Black Rhythm," in *Music and the Racial Imagination*, ed. Ronald Radano and Philip V. Bohlman (University of Chicago Press, 2000), 460.

48. Stoever, *Sonic Color Line*, 6; Radano, "Hot Fantasies," 473.
49. Magee, *Uncrowned King*, 27.
50. Virginia Sterilization Act of 1924, Virginia General Assembly, SB281. This act was upheld in a 1927 Supreme Court case, *Buck v. Bell*, in which the Court ruled in favor of the compulsory sterilization of "unfit" individuals. *Buck v. Bell* was also cited at the Nuremberg trials by lawyers to defend Nazi scientists whose actions led to the sterilization of 375,000 Jews. For more, see Adam Cohen, *Imbeciles: The Supreme Court, American Eugenics, and the Sterilization of Carrie Buck* (Penguin Press, 2016), 11. It is also worth noting that the Immigration Act of 1924, also called the Johnson–Reed Act, which severely limited the number of immigrants from Asia and Eastern Europe, passed that same year.
51. Gregory Michael Dorr, "Assuring America's Place in the Sun: Ivey Foreman Lewis and the Teaching of Eugenics at the University of Virginia, 1915–1953," *Journal of Southern History* 66, no. 2 (May 2000): 285.
52. For more on this topic, see: Stephanie DeLane Doktor, "How a White Supremacist Became Famous for His Black Music: John Powell and *Rhapsodie nègre* (1918)," *American Music* 38, no. 4 (Winter 2020): 395–427; Richard Hofstadter, *Social Darwinism in American Thought*, reprint, with a new introduction by Eric Foner (Beacon Press, 1992); Lee D. Baker, *From Savage to Negro: Anthropology and the Construction of Race, 1896–1954* (University of California, 1998), 35; Jonathan Peter Spiro, *Defending the Master Race: Conservation, Eugenics, and the Legacy of Madison Grant* (University of Vermont Press, 2009); Cohen, *Imbeciles*.
53. Philip A. Ewell, "Music Theory and the White Racial Frame," *Music Theory Online* 26, no. 2 (September 2020), https://mtosmt.org/issues/mto.20.26.2/mto.20.26.2.ewell.html; Alexander William Cowan, "Unsound: A Cultural History of Music and Eugenics" (PhD diss., Harvard University, 2023); Stoever, *Sonic Color Line*, 4.
54. Wald, *How the Beatles*, 76–77 and 85. For the song, see Paul Whiteman, "Whispering," Spotify, August 23, 1920, https://open.spotify.com/track/4gQckZoYAFSrkXLet6sKG6?si=8e2f76af6aca4952.
55. For "San," see Paul Whiteman, "San – Paul Whiteman and His Orch. Featuring Bix Beiderbecke, Tram, Jimmy Dorsey and Bill Challis," YouTube, January 12, 1928, https://www.youtube.com/watch?v=90z3VjB7zow; and for "Changes," see Paul Whiteman, "Changes (feat. Bing Crosby)," https://open.spotify.com/track/2CyRmQ6TQsAG1fwQQTLneh?si=6e39061760934759 (Accessed July 24, 2024).
56. For an analysis of "San" and "Changes," see my chapter "Arranging Whiteness: The Gendered and Racialized Sounds of Early Jazz," in *The Oxford Handbook*

of Arrangement Studies, ed. Ryan Bañagale (Oxford University Press, forthcoming), https://doi.org/10.1093/oxfordhb/9780190061869.013.13.

57. Notably, Whiteman courted many Black listeners. In some circles, he was admired for making jazz mainstream and demonstrating Black music's artistic capabilities by pairing it with classical music culture. See: Christi Jay Wells (fka Christopher Jay Wells), "'The Ace of His Race': Paul Whiteman's Early Critical Reception in the Black Press," *Jazz & Culture* 1 (January 2018): 77–103.
58. Don Rayno, *Paul Whiteman: Pioneer in American Music, Volume 1, 1890–1930*, (Scarecrow Press, 2003), 50; Paul Whiteman, "What is Jazz Doing to American Music?" *The Etude* 42, no. 8 (August 1924): 523.
59. Thomas A. DeLong, *Pops: Paul Whiteman, King of Jazz* (New Century, 1983), 4 and 84.
60. Rayno, *Paul Whiteman: Pioneer*, 189.
61. Rayno, *Paul Whiteman: Pioneer*, 222.
62. Magee, *Uncrowned King*, 7; Clifford J. Doerksen, "'Serving the Masses, Not the Classes': Station WHN, Pioneer of Commercial Broadcasting of the 1920s," *Journal of Radio Studies* 6, no. 1 (1999): 87–88.
63. Magee, *Uncrowned King*, 7.
64. By the late 1930s and early 1940s, monographs about jazz's history and stylistic development materialized. These became more common in the 1960s and 1970s, as this Black American music became something you could study in higher education. The University of North Texas offered the very first jazz performance degree in 1947. For more on the rise of jazz studies in higher education, see: Kenneth E. Prouty, "The History of Jazz Education: A Critical Reassessment," *Journal of Historical Research in Music Education* 26, no. 2 (April 2005): 79–100; Ken Prouty, "Jazz Education: Historical and Critical Perspectives," in *The Routledge Companion to Jazz Studies*, ed. Nicholas Gebhardt, Nichole Rustin-Paschal, and Tony Whyton, 45–53 (Routledge, 2019); and Ken Prouty, *Learning Jazz: Jazz Education, History, and Public Pedagogy* (University Press of Mississippi, 2023).
65. Extensive analysis appears in one of the first studies dedicated solely to this time period (Gunther Schuller's *Early Jazz*, published in 1968), and one man, Walter C. Allen, published an entire book on the bandleader in 1973 entitled *Hendersonia: The Music of Fletcher Henderson and His Musicians: A Bio-Discography*. Gunther Schuller, *Early Jazz: Its Roots and Musical Development* (Oxford University Press, 1968); Allen, *Hendersonia*.
66. Schuller, *Early Jazz*, 253; Magee, *Uncrowned King*, 27.
67. Scott DeVeaux and Gary Giddins, *Jazz*, 2nd ed. (W. W. Norton, 2015), 107–129.

68. I have made similar points and summarized similar scholarship in the following forthcoming book chapter: Stephanie Doktor, "Arranging Whiteness: The Gendered and Racialized Sounds of Early Jazz," in the *Oxford Handbook of Arrangement Studies*, ed. Ryan Bañagale (Oxford University Press, forthcoming). Also see: Mark Tucker, "In Search of Will Vodery," *Black Music Research Journal* 16, no. 1 (Spring 1996), 123; John Wriggle, *Blue Rhythm Fantasy: Big Band Jazz Arranging in the Swing Era* (University of Illinois Press, 2016), 1.
69. Magee, *Uncrowned King*, 27.
70. Scott DeVeaux, "Constructing the Jazz Tradition: Jazz Historiography," *Black American Literature Forum* 25, no. 3 (Autumn 1991), 530.
71. To listen to "Montero (Call Me By Your Name)," see Lil Nas X, "Montero (Call Me By Your Name)," music video, YouTube, March 26, 2021, https://www.youtube.com/watch?v=6swmTBVI83k; and to listen to "Industry Baby," see Lil Nas X, Jack Harlow – Industry Baby," music video, YouTube, July 23, 2021, https://www.youtube.com/watch?v=UTHLKHL_whs.
72. See Michelle Alexander, *The New Jim Crow: Mass Incarceration in the Age of Colorblindness* (New Press, 2010); *13th*, directed by Ava DuVernay (Netflix, 2016), https://www.netflix.com/watch/80091741?source=35; Angela J. Davis, ed., *Policing the Black Man: Arrest, Prosecution, and Imprisonment* (Pantheon, 2017); Angela Y. Davis, Gina Dent, Erica R. Meiners, and Beth E. Richie, *Abolition. Feminism. Now.*, Abolitionist Papers 2 (Haymarket Books, 2022).
73. Chris Molanphy, "Introducing the King of Hip-Hop," *Rolling Stone*, August 15, 2011, https://www.rollingstone.com/music/music-news/introducing-the-king-of-hip-hop-101033/.
74. Katie Atkinson, "Tyler, the Creator Calls Out Grammy Categories: 'Urban' is Just 'A Politically Correct Way to Say the N-Word,'" Billboard, January 26, 2020, https://www.billboard.com/music/awards/tyler-the-creator-grammys-best-rap-album-win-backstage-comments-categories-urban-8549244/.
75. Time stamps may differ slightly depending on the recording speed and streaming media.

CHAPTER TWO

SPONTANEOUS COMPOSITION AND CHARLES MINGUS'S "SCENES IN THE CITY"

Vilde Aaslid

When I first heard the combination of jazz and poetry, I was in my first semester of my master's degree in musicology. Much of my work up to that point had involved an intensive study of song, focused on the expressive combination of music and language. I was used to thinking carefully about how music and words interacted in that context, but when I heard a poet performing with jazz I felt immediately that I had almost no tools for understanding what I was hearing. This initial bewilderment morphed swiftly into curiosity, and I found myself asking question after question about what I was hearing. How could the musicians be reacting meaningfully to the poet's words when poetry often encourages us to sit and ponder slowly as we grapple with it? If musicians are improvising and the poet is reading, what kind of process is this? Who is controlling how this piece unfolds and how? And if I listen to how this works, what can I learn about all the other ways that language and music come together? These questions drew me like a current, pulling me into a research trajectory that extends into today.

This research has taken me on a lively path of investigation that follows the work through decades and into our current jazz scene. Throughout this journey, I constantly stay aware of my fundamental outsider status. I am not a poet, and I do not play jazz, so in many ways I come at these practices as an outsider. As a white woman who often writes about Black music, it is imperative that I remember: this music does not belong to me. I am ever aware of the ways that my writing about it has the potential to do harm as well as good. This is not a one-and-done process; as the external world's racial politics develop, so too does the relationship between my research and me. Part of this process involves asking: why am I writing this essay, and what do I have to offer here? My hope with this essay is partly that the curiosity that sparked my own research fire will serve as kindling for your own wondering about some of the big questions that run through this essay: what does it mean to compose? What kind of thing is music and what kind of thing is language? Why do we bring them together and what happens when we do?

> *If you like Beethoven, Bach or Brahms, that's okay. They were all pencil composers. I always wanted to be a spontaneous composer.*
>
> —Charles Mingus

The late 1950s was a legendarily rich time for jazz in New York City. While the early strains of rock'n'roll filled the radio airwaves, the clubs of Manhattan were host to some of the most iconic figures in jazz history: Miles Davis, Billie Holiday, John Coltrane, Thelonious Monk, Dizzy Gillespie, and on and on. Among these titans was the bassist, composer, and bandleader Charles Mingus. As the jazz scene dug deeply into the developing styles of hard bop and cool jazz, Mingus, who has been called "the avant-garde's reluctant father," continued to stretch in new directions.[1] Throughout his lifetime Mingus had a fluctuating relationship with what he called "pencil composition," and the late 1950s found him most deeply invested in an approach to composition based in improvisation and orality. He called it "spontaneous composition."

Mingus traversed New York's many diverse cultural fields, and in the same years when he was working through his ideas of spontaneous composition, he was also in close contact with two significant new movements. First of these was the coalescing of a core group of American experimentalists prompting a reconsideration of some of the most basic principles of what "composition" means. Mingus's musings on spontaneous composition were happening alongside the work of figures like John Cage and Earle Brown. At the same time, Beat Generation poets led a faddish explosion of poetry-read-to-jazz performances. Coffee houses and jazz clubs became the hip new venues for poetry readings, and the jazz press lit up with debates about the merits of combining spoken language with jazz music. Mingus was at the center of the press's coverage of this movement and several of his late 1950s recordings feature spoken word.

In what follows, we will listen closely to one of these projects, "Scenes in the City" from 1957, to hear how Mingus's spontaneous composition model works in the practice of combining music and language. The conversation about what counts as "composition" was always political for Mingus. As we listen to "Scenes in the City" we will place it within and against the racial politics of the two New York scenes described above. When discussing jazz, both the Beats and the experimentalists exhibited dehumanizing primitivism. One way of understanding "Scenes in the City" is as Mingus's creative intervention against these views. Throughout this essay, we will trace the way Mingus engages with two pairs of ideas that we sometimes imagine as being in opposition to each other. The first of these is improvisation and composition; what do we see as the distinction between these two processes and why do we draw the line where we draw it? The second is music and language; how do humans go about expressing in these different media and is the boundary between them as clear as we might first imagine?

JAZZ POETRY AND THE BUBBLE OF 1957–1959

Jazz and poetry have had a long and varied connection in Black expressive culture of the twentieth and twenty-first centuries. In its nascent days, jazz developed alongside the blues, and that genre's lyrical structure—a poetic form—contributed to the musical foundation of jazz. Poets, in turn, drew on jazz, especially during the artistic flourishing of the Harlem Renaissance when writers like Zora Neale Hurston and Langston Hughes described the music in startling prose and poetry. In 1928, prominent African American sociologist Charles S. Johnson wrote that his era's jazz poetry was "a venture in the new, bold rhythms characteristic of the music."[2] The Black Arts Movement of the late 1960s found poets like Amiri Baraka and Jayne Cortez working with musicians to create their urgent political art. Beyond these moments of heightened contact, the history of jazz has within it a continuous engagement with poetry. Scholars of the intersection of music and literature in Black expressive culture have argued for understanding this relationship as "an approach to aesthetics that resists any easy distinction between 'writing' and 'music,' instead viewing both as components in a broader sphere of art making and performance."[3] To hear what this combination sounds like in contemporary practices, we can visit with the videos linked here. In one, poet Nathaniel Mackey reads with bassist Vattel Cherry in an improvised conversation.[4] In the other, saxophonist Matana Roberts creates an experimental blend of poetry, solo saxophone, and film as part of their long-running *Coin Coin* project.[5]

Despite the richness of this history, one brief non-representative period in jazz and poetry's combined history has had an outsized presence in the form's history: the poetry-read-to-jazz bubble of 1957–1959. You might already be familiar with the visual signifiers of this briefly popular form of jazz poetry: a smoky café, a small jazz backing band, and a beret-wearing white poet at the microphone, perhaps with a set of bongos nearby. Driven by the largely white countercultural youth followers of the Beat poets, the poetry-read-to-jazz fad of the late 1950s became a facet of the mainstream culture's representation of the youth movement through the figure of the "beatnik." The trend began in the spring of 1957 in San Francisco, with a series of performances by poets Kenneth Rexroth and Lawrence Ferlinghetti with "jazz backing" at a club called The Cellar. By January 1958, the prominent jazz magazine *Down Beat* was reporting on the impending arrival of Beat poet Jack Kerouac in New York, for an engagement at the Village Vanguard. The following months brought a flurry of coverage as performances of poetry with jazz spread through the city. But just as suddenly as it emerged, the poetry-read-to-jazz trend faded from the scene, continuing to exist only in parody. As early as April 1958, a reader of the jazz periodical *Metronome* wrote a letter to the editor saying, "having once experienced a Poetry and Jazz session some years ago, I was shocked to find out by reading *Metronome* that the idea still persists."[6] By 1964, the trend had become so mainstream that Mattel was making beatnik-inspired dolls with winged eyeliner and pull-string recorded catchphrases like "I dig that crazy beat, yeah!"

Many jazz critics were skeptical of the Beat-driven movement from the start. In November 1957, even before the jazz poetry fad had arrived in New York, critic Ralph Gleason wrote, "Mostly the poets are slumming. Jazz already has an audience and they don't. They're cashing in on the jazz audience but they won't learn anything about jazz."[7] Another critic, Nat Hentoff, wrote that "jazz in this context has been reduced to a gimmick."[8] As was the case with many of the countercultural movements of the time, the relationship between white youth and Black expressive culture was exploitative, reductive, and primitivist, as we can read in this 1957 letter from a *Down Beat* reader: "True, jazzmen are often suspicious of intellectual things. Just as poets likewise (except in a case such as Allen Ginsberg or Kenneth Ford) ignore the forms and virility of jazz."[9] Meanwhile, even the jazz critics with some awareness of the racial politics at work still seemed to write from a place of ignorance about the longer history of jazz and poetry. Gleason, for example, appeared to forget the entire Harlem Renaissance when he wrote: "Not until a poet comes along who learns what jazz is all about and then writes poetry will there be any merger."[10]

A quick listen to one recording from the 1957–1959 bubble will help ground this discussion in sound. Jack Kerouac, perhaps the most prominent of the Beat Generation figures, recorded *Blues and Haikus* with the two saxophonists Zoot Sims and Al Cohn in 1958. On the album the trio takes a variety of approaches to combining music and poetry. I will focus on the track "Poems from the unpublished 'Book of Blues'" as it captures several common characteristics from the broader movement.[11] At the start of the track, we can hear Kerouac telling the engineer "I would like them to play behind me while I am reading" already establishing the music's positionality in relation to the poetry: behind. And then, more hesitatingly, he asks, "Can you hear me while they're playing?" The engineer's answer of yes gives another layer to the music's position: below. From this below and behind place, the two saxophonists seem to do their best to accommodate Kerouac's verse through a meandering rendition of the jazz standard "Don't Get Around Much Anymore." At the opening, the poet and musicians try to give each other space, exchanging lead roles. But following the promising opening, the trio devolves into an unfortunate cacophony, where the music is hard to hear over Kerouac's loud, reverbed reading and the poetry clashes with the saxophonists playing. The process of jazz improvisation has often been characterized as "saying something," and this track has the quality of too many people saying something at the same time.[12]

Generally speaking, the Beat-era recordings make little attempt to craft a meaningful relationship between the music and poetry, and the movement has been dismissed by many as having been more focused on the *idea* of jazz than on actual artistic conversation.[13] The recordings from this time reflect the shallowness of that engagement; even Kenneth Rexroth, one of the San Francisco poets responsible for starting the bubble, later described the effect as fundamentally disjointed: "The poet ended up sounding like he was hawking fish from a street corner. All the musicians wanted to do was blow. Like, 'Man, go ahead and read your poems but we gotta blow.'"[14] Unfortunately, the most faddish characteristics of this period continue to shape history's understanding of early jazz poetry intersection. As poetry scholar Sascha Feinstein has noted,

> To this day, the term "jazz poet" generally conjures up images of the hipster figures with dated jargon and self-conscious personas. Ironically, the stereotypes linked with the least successful jazz poetry performances from the late fifties still constitute the general image of jazz and poetry, as though no other relationship exists. For over thirty years, the most-pretentious qualities of jazz poetry have remained representative and have hurt rather than helped the diverse efforts by poets from the sixties to the present who have been interested in the union between poetry and jazz.[15]

But while present day histories might focus on the hipster characters of the bubble, the jazz press's coverage from the time points to the prominence of another figure altogether: Charles Mingus. In November 1957, Atlantic records advertised Mingus's *The Clown* in multiple jazz publications under the headline "The Beat generation," saying further that "this is the generation-of-the-beat and it is inspiring a new literature and a new music."[16] In January 1958, Mingus was framed as core to the jazz poetry narrative:

> The Half Note, skippered by Mike Canterino [...] struggled for life for months. It remained for Charlie Mingus and his Jazz Workshop to bring in the poetry-readers-to-jazz, following a formula successful in San Francisco, to make the spot. At year's end, Canterino was paying his way out of the hole, and had knocked down a wall to increase his seating capacity.[17]

Mingus's interest in poetry was anything but faddish; his writings and recordings show a lifelong poetic orientation.[18] He also operated with a savvy awareness of how stories become histories. In the same period during which he was splashed through the pages of the jazz press as a leader in the jazz-with-poetry bubble, Mingus was also at work constructing the narrative of his identity as a composer and what that meant for his place in the cultural hierarchy.

SPONTANEOUS COMPOSITION

The term "composer" has a complicated position in jazz. Jazz is created through a range of activities: notation of ideas by a single person, arrangement of existing musical ideas, collaborative workshopping of material, and in-the-moment creativity of improvisation.[19] Focusing on the compositional process can help us understand the work of musicians like Duke Ellington, for whom composition was an important part of their creative lives; however, doing so comes at the risk of overemphasizing composition's place in the jazz creation process and reifying "the composer" as the sole source of music. Jazz criticism that focuses on composition often assesses the music using criteria imported from the European classical tradition, devaluing arranging and improvisation.[20] We are focusing on composition here not in order to elevate it above other forms of musical creation, but because it was an idea that mattered tremendously to Charles Mingus. As Nichole Rustin-Paschal writes, "Mingus's major priority was to establish himself as a composer; Duke Ellington was the barometer by which he measured himself."[21]

As we saw from the quote at the start of this essay, Mingus staked a claim for himself as a "spontaneous composer," in contrast to the "pencil composition" of the European classical tradition. Mingus developed his ideas about spontaneous composition in a time when he was frequently participating in public conversations about "third stream" music, a movement led by Gunther Schuller that sought to blend the aesthetic principles of jazz and classical music.[22] At the same time, Mingus was also involved in experimental music sessions held by avant-garde composer Edgard Varèse and attended by core experimentalists like John Cage.[23] There, and doubtless in plenty of other undocumented encounters, Mingus would have come into contact with the avant-garde's radical restructuring of the relationships between composer, notation, performer, and work. As George Lewis has demonstrated, Cage and his close associates framed their ideas about indeterminacy as distinct from, even in opposition to, those of jazz improvisation.[24] Their distinction reinforced racialized genre hierarchies that separated jazz from "serious" music. Primitivist ideas permeated their views of jazz improvisation and possibly even inflected how

Varèse structured the sessions that Mingus participated in.[25] We can hear in Mingus's spontaneous/pencil distinction his ideological sparring with multiple veins of classically defined "composition."

Mingus's vehicle for his spontaneous composition was, in the 1950s and early 1960s, his Jazz Workshop ensemble. Conceptualized as an experimental collaborative structure with Mingus at the helm, the ensemble explored the oral creation of jazz through their practices. Mingus required rigor and commitment from his group and stories circulate of members jokingly calling it the "Jazz Sweatshop." He demanded much of his players, and when they failed him, Mingus berated his band members, sometimes even in front of their audiences. Musically, too, Mingus kept them on their toes. According to pianist and arranger Sy Johnson:

> When he felt the band had become too facile—just swinging along—he'd destroy that ambience because he wanted us to *think* about what we were playing. He'd suddenly switch from four to six beats to the bar, and it was like slipping on a piece of ice on the street. You'd fall on your ass. But you'd surely be thinking. Mingus gave you *resistance*. He never thought his function was to support the soloist but rather to stir him up.[26]

The ensemble that emerged from Mingus's unpredictable and challenging leadership was a crucial contribution to his critically acclaimed work from the time.

In the mid-1950s, Mingus's compositional approach was to stay entirely off the written page. When he worked with the Jazz Workshop he transmitted his compositions orally, singing or playing parts for his ensemble members. It was a painstaking and sometimes frustrating process, but Mingus believed that this orality allowed for the stylistic contributions of each of his bandmates. As he wrote in his liner notes to the album *Pithecanthropus Erectus* (1956):

> My whole conception with my present Jazz Workshop group deals with nothing written. [...] I play them the 'framework' on piano so that they are all familiar with my interpretation and feeling and with the scale and

> chord progression to be used. Each man's own particular style is taken into consideration, both in ensemble and in solos. For instance, they are given different rows of notes to use against each chord but they choose their own notes and play them in their own style, from scales as well as chords, except where a particular mood is indicated. In this way, I find it possible to keep my own compositional flavor in the pieces and yet to allow the musicians more individual freedom in the creation of their group lines and solos.[27]

Some scholars have interpreted this move as fundamentally egalitarian, distributing creative agency among ensemble members.[28] Others see it as simply shifting Mingus's authorial (and authoritative) role to a different format.[29] But certainly, like his counterparts in the Cage circles, Mingus was thinking carefully about the relationship between notation and a composer's ideas:[30]

> [...] a jazz musician, although he might read all the notes and play them with jazz feeling, inevitably introduces his own **individual** expression rather than what the composer intended. It is amazing how many ways a four-bar phrase of four beats per measure can be interpreted![31]

Contrary to what one might expect, Mingus's choice to convey his compositions without the use of notation did not lead to him simplifying his approach to form. Eschewing the theme–solos–theme structure common to much jazz of the period, Mingus often used what Andrew Homzy has termed "plastic form," and Mingus himself called "extended form."[32] He built compositions with distinct sections but adjusted how his group moved through these sections in every performance, depending on the mood of the soloist, the scene in the venue, or whatever other factors were at play. Scott Saul describes the process:

> Sections of a composition would be elongated, compressed, or recombined, their underlying rhythms radically altered through stop-time, background riffs, new bass vamps—and much of this would be signaled

as the composition was being enacted. The oral instruction before the gig was followed by a collaborative environment during the gig, where the musicians would cue each other in the next section spontaneously.[33]

We can hear one example of Mingus using extended form in his 1956 recording of "Pithecanthropus Erectus." Here, the Jazz Workshop alternates between tightly orchestrated sixteen-bar sections and expansive collectively improvised passages. Each of these sections features different approaches to timbre and texture, meant to reflect the narrative of early humans' development; Mingus calls the piece a "tone poem" in the liner notes.

Mingus, characteristically, had a broad view of how this compositional mode functioned, including processes beyond the confines of a single piece. "The greatness of jazz is that it is an art of the moment, it is so particularly through improvisation, but also, in my music, through successive relation of one composition to another."[34] Composition expanded to include the events of an entire evening's performance. In his formulation, then, Mingus's spontaneous composition took place not only in the original creation of the musical material, but also in the expansion, contraction, and rearrangement of that material. It was using this method that Mingus brought his musical approach to the jazz poetry movement, both in live practice in clubs like the Half Note and in recorded pieces like "Scenes in the City."

"A COLLOQUIAL DREAM"/"SCENES IN THE CITY" AND EXTENDED FORM

In August 1957, Mingus gathered a group of his regular collaborators for a recording session. Among the tracks recorded that day was "A Colloquial Dream," a narrative combination of spoken words and music told from the perspective of a Harlem-dwelling music lover.[35] Lonnie Elder, the actor and playwright who first conceived and wrote the text for the piece, performed as narrator.[36] Delays from the record company meant that the material recorded that day went unreleased until 1962, when much of it came out as *Tijuana Moods.* "A Colloquial Dream," however, did not make the cut and remained unreleased until 2001. In October 1957, just a few months after the *Tijuana Moods* session, Mingus rerecorded "A Colloquial Dream," with actor Melvin Stewart performing the narration. This new recording, now renamed "Scenes in the City," was released a few years later on *A Modern Jazz Symposium of Poetry and Music* (1959). Despite the album's title, "Scenes" is the only track on the record that features spoken text.

Why did Mingus rerecord "A Colloquial Dream"/"Scenes in the City" while letting the other tracks that would become *Tijuana Moods* sit unreleased for five years? Although Mingus often recorded and released multiple versions of his pieces, renaming as necessary to avoid legal trouble, the Colloquial/Scenes pair is unusual for the tight timeframe between the two recordings. The switch in narrator suggests that perhaps Mingus was unhappy with the performance on the first recording and took the delay as an opportunity to rerecord. But a likelier explanation is that Mingus felt that there was a time-sensitive nature to the recording, and wanted it released immediately. As scholar Anthony Reed has pointed out, the piece fits within Mingus's broader experiments in multimedia work, a project that he was especially focused on in the last years of the 1950s.[37] Separately, as the jazz poetry bubble expanded around him, Mingus, always a shrewd cultural observer, would likely have predicted the boom/bust nature of the trend. Having a shelved track meant a missed opportunity to both benefit from the swirling publicity and potentially guide the form's development from the position of a core figure in the movement. Mingus was working through his ideas about both composition and texted music in pieces like "Scenes," and it seems clear that he wanted them to be heard.

A brief side-by-side comparison of "A Colloquial Dream" and "Scenes in the City" helps illustrate the balance of fixed and improvised approaches in the Jazz Workshop process. At first hearing, the two recordings strongly resemble each other; however, closer attention reveals that while similar in contour and mood, the exact musical details are improvised. Section by section, "Scenes in the City" and "Colloquial Dream" follow the same pattern, but within these sections there are small variations that emerge from Mingus's compositional method and the structured freedom of his extended form.

The second section of the piece, immediately following a five-second-long opening passage, provides a helpful illustration of the improvisatory flexibility in Mingus's structure. Both recordings feature solo bowed bass in this passage and both are relatively sparse in texture. But the pitches and timing of the segments of melody are entirely different between the two. In "Scenes in the City" Mingus enters nearly immediately following the horn section, playing melodic lines in the middle to high register. In "A Colloquial Dream," Mingus waits significantly longer to enter, and when he does it is in a much lower register. He pauses longer between his fragments, and they are less melodic than in the other recording. The two recordings share some key characteristics here—bowed solo bass, sparse, quiet—but are otherwise distinct.

The similarities between the two recordings go far beyond Mingus's own improvised sections. As an example from another member of the ensemble, see the transcription in Figure 2.1, which captures the same moment in the two recordings, each played on the alto saxophone.

The pitch sets and contours are very similar between the two recordings, but not identical. This kind of variation is typical of the two recordings, reflecting the oral method of composition. Mingus would likely have sung an approximate melody line or perhaps made a suggestion like "Play a C Locrian stepwise thing" and left the details to the improviser.

With nearly the exact same personnel, it is unsurprising that "Scenes in the City" and "Colloquial Dream" are so similar, but the small variations

Figure 2.1. Alto saxophone transitions [5:12] "Scenes in the City"; [5:32] "A Colloquial Dream."

demonstrate the degree of openness in this work. This improvisational space creates, necessarily, a position of listening for everyone in the ensemble. The narrator and the musicians depend on cues from each other to time their progression through the work. Mingus biographer Brian Priestley calls out the performance on "Scenes" as an especially successful example of Mingus's band from the period, characterizing their playing as "brilliantly self-assured in their handling of the periodic structure and frequent time changes."[38]

Let's turn now to the details of "Scenes in the City" in order to listen for how Mingus's spontaneous composition approach helped him successfully navigate the challenges of combining spoken text and improvised music. His approach here is certainly not the only method of doing so—the scores of fantastic jazz/poetry records from later in the 1960s offer plenty alternatives that prioritize more space for improvisation—but during the late 1950s bubble, his work is a rare success. Mingus used "extended form" as described above, creating sections of music that function as small-scale environments for short segments of text. Movement between these sections was cued, either by Mingus or members of the ensemble and the music in the sections could expand or contract depending on the improvised events. In this responsive environment, the narrator became a full member of the Jazz Workshop ensemble, receiving as well as giving the cues that would move the group spontaneously through Mingus's composed form. Table 2.1 provides an overview of the piece's sectional divisions, and you can track the following discussion using the parenthetical references to the figure's "Section" column.

Narrator Melvin Stewart describes the text of "Scenes" as

> an examination of a guy from Harlem and his relationship to jazz. It shows what jazz can mean to someone who's not basically a musician but who 'lives on that music' a lot [...] Jazz helps the man in this piece hear *himself*, the way he is and feels, and every note becomes a part of him as he is now and as he'd like the world to be.[39]

Table 2.1. Structural guide for "Scenes in the City"

Time	Section	Opening line	Lyrical themes	Musical characteristics
0:00–0:05	Opening	–	–	Busy, swinging, full ensemble
0:06–0:53	A1	*Well, here I am*	Downtown, jazz, alienation	Solo, melancholy bass with intermittent percussion, free rhythm
0:54–1:19	Transition 1	*I once wanted to be an actor*	Aspirations, poverty	Unaccompanied muted trumpet, cymbal roll
1:19–2:13	A2	*You see, I love jazz music*	Music and beauty comparison with women	Muted trumpet ballad, slow sweet bass and piano
2:14–2:47	Transition 2	*Now catch this!*	–	Busy, swinging, full ensemble
2:48–4:33	B	*Now, here I am standing at my window*	Chaos in Harlem apartment building, desire for quiet and "cool"	Swinging, shouting, driving groove, dense
4:34–4:50	Transition 3	*Madam may I please get in there soon*	Asking for entrance to the shared bathroom	Groove dissipates, diminuendo,
4:51–5:46	C	*I guess I'm the only man in the world*	Mother's relationship to jazz, list of jazz greats	Arhythmic spurts of mostly solo instrumental responses to the text

(Continued)

Table 2.1. continued

Time	Section	Opening line	Lyrical themes	Musical characteristics
5:47–5:59	Transition 4	*I played her some Monk*	Monk's music bringing Mother into jazz	Hints of "Round Midnight," walking bass starts up
6:00–7:14	D1	–	–	Solos over changes to "Round Midnight"
7:15–7:23	Transition 5	–	–	Groove slows, cymbal roll with brushes
7:24–8:01	D2	–	–	Open, alternation between trumpet, saxophone, and drums
8:02	D3	–	–	Driving groove
8:27	D4	–	–	Slow blues, trombone solo
9:22–9:59	E1	*Blues walked in*	The multiplicity of the blues	Blend of some of the previous, ride cymbals, cadential
10:00–11:19	E2	*And with the blues, whether I like it or not*	Poverty, hope, comparison with women	Return to muted trumpet ballad from A2

The narration has four main sections, each spoken from a first-person perspective but with shifts between internal/external reflection as well as movement through Manhattan. It opens downtown (Sections A1 and A2 on Table 2.1), with the narrator listening to and reflecting on the music he loves: jazz. The second section (B) shifts uptown to Harlem and depicts the narrator's non-musical daily life. A brief third section (C and Transition 4) describes the narrator's mother's conversion into a jazz fan, and the whole piece closes (sections E1 and E2) with an introspective reflection on life, hope, and the blues.[40]

Mingus vividly depicts the different environments of the poem and the shifts between uptown/downtown and external/internal. His settings are relatively straightforward, creating moods in the music that match those of the narration. A few selected examples from the twelve-minute piece will help illustrate this technique. Mingus opens the piece with a bustling, full-ensemble passage with horns moving in rhythmic unison through dissonant voicings, evoking the busy eponymous city. This passage frames the whole piece, establishing the New York City location and serving as a kind of refrain as it reappears through the piece, a reminder that even when the narrator has his internal daydreams he is still within the context of the city. At [0:56] the trumpet plays a wistful ballad just before the narrator speaks to us directly: "That's jazz music you're listening to." The content of the narration explicitly connects with the music we hear, in a sense transporting us into the scene along with the narrator. Later, in a passage describing the narrator's chaotic life in Harlem, Mingus scores the scene with a raucous approach [2:45]. Frenzied and dense, the music makes visceral the intensity of the narrator's description.

In one sense, the relationship between music and text here is familiar, functioning almost like a stage set for a theatrical production. But unlike a static backdrop, this musical setting is dynamic. If the narrator raised his voice in a passage, the musicians could work within their sectional parameters to respond and react, connecting the moment-to-moment developments in the text's performance with the music. This responsivity elides some of the divisions between how music and spoken language express, highlighting the expressive features that the two media share: volume, articulation, phrasing, and so on.

Mingus often marks the transition between his sections with a sonic cue for the listener, indicating that we are entering a new setting. Some of these transitions are themselves depictive; for example, as the narration moves from downtown to uptown, Mingus's ensemble accelerates rapidly (Transition 2), bringing to mind the long speedy ride under Central Park that this commute entails in real life. Others are more abstract; in the shift from the Harlem scene to the narrator's reminiscing about his mother and jazz, Mingus marks the section division by slowing the tempo and finally landing on a full-ensemble unison with a cymbal roll (Transition 3). These section markers show Mingus attending to the text's topical divisions and highlighting them through his musical setting.

The sectional markers also point to Mingus's careful attention to the shape and flow of the sonic contour of "Scenes." In addition to musical variables like dynamics and texture, Mingus also uses extended form to vary the degree of focus on music or text. Once again, the very start of the piece offers a good example. After the initial busy opening, the horns stop suddenly and into the silence enters narrator Stewart with, "Well, here I am." The text continues with a description of the narrator, "sitting on a high barstool holding my dreams up to the sound of jazz music," and his splintered life between his mundane residence uptown and his artistic home downtown. Mingus's plaintive solo bass improvisation pauses between fragments, subtly setting the melancholic mood while giving Stewart space to establish the character of the narrator. Here, the focus is strongly on the text, but with echoes and suggestions from the music. But later, Mingus carves out space for a focus on the musical contribution to the piece. Two and a half minutes in, roughly overlapping with Transition 2's trip uptown, Mingus takes a full forty-five seconds without any spoken narration. He layers the horns in one by one, musically announcing each member of the ensemble. The interlude lets the band members stretch out and reminds the listener that this is a jazz piece as well as a narration. It also gives some breathing space to the listener as we sit with the text we have heard so far.

At times Mingus brings the music and text into intentional conflict. In the Harlem section of the text, as the narrator describes the chaos of his uptown home, the noise from the neighbors, waiting for the washroom, and avoiding the landlady, the musical setting competes for attention with the text (B). As Mingus walks an ostinato chord, his drummer Dannie Richmond keeps an up-tempo groove from the preceding musical interlude. The piano and horns interject short bluesy fragments. The frenzied and dense music overwhelms the text, as the trumpet squeals dissonantly and Mingus and his band mates yell theatrically in the background. Instead of carefully underscoring the text or framing it with gentle musical conversation, here Mingus drowns out the narrator, using his approach to text and music balance to depict the commotion described in the text.

In his sensitive reading of "Scenes in the City," Mingus shifts constantly—in texture, in dynamics, and in his treatment of the narration. At times, he tiptoes musically with his ensemble, making way for the denser text. At other points he puts the musicians center-stage, granting expressive space to the musical component of the work. These interludes allow time to contemplate the text, avoiding the kind of semantic overload sometimes experienced in jazz poetry collaborations. Mingus's composition creates sections of music that support the text, while the improvisational elements require all members of the ensemble, including the narrator, to stay dynamically connected to each other. Mingus, in typical form, kept tight controls on his ensemble and scripted a musical response to the poetry that allowed for both his compositional response to the text and for the core improvisational component of jazz. In doing so, he found a way of integrating improvisation into a texted work: his extended form.

MINGUS THE SELF-HISTORIAN

Throughout his life, Mingus wrote with an eye toward the future. In his interviews, his liner notes, and especially in his autobiography, he demonstrated a shrewd awareness of how his words might shape his legacy.[41] And it seems as though he thought we would need some guidance to get it right, his words offering ready-packaged narratives of his contributions. This self-historizing was related to his civil rights work; he often wrote against the racialized genre policing and primitivist discourses that were all too common in the jazz press of the time. One way we can hear "Scenes in the City" is as an artistic extension of his interest in framing his own legacy. By rerecording "Scenes" after "A Colloquial Dream" was shelved, Mingus demonstrated his commitment to getting the piece released. Pushing back against a jazz press that viewed jazz and poetry as a shallow fad with no artistic value, here Mingus offered a piece with a thoughtful and effective combination of spoken word and jazz music. And against the primitivist views of a rapidly consolidating experimentalist scene, Mingus offered an example of a mode of composition that incorporated within it the multiple creative modalities of jazz.

In short, I hear "Scenes" as a kind of intervention into the multiple scenes that Mingus moved across and between in his rich and idiosyncratic artistic life in late 1950s New York City. Tracing the piece through these different intersections reminds us that we must attend to the boundaries of our narratives. Jazz stories are all too often told as though the genre we use to describe the music also somehow draws borders around the possible experiences in jazz musicians' lives. For Mingus, and for many other musicians before and since, a full understanding requires us to listen across these boundaries.

NOTES

1. Mingus had a complex relationship with the avant-garde. He famously criticized some of its most prominent proponents, but quietly deployed many avant-garde techniques in his own work. For a deep consideration of Mingus's position in relation to avant-garde jazz see: Salim Washington, "'All the Things You Could Be by Now': *Charles Mingus Presents Charles Mingus* and the Limits of Avant-Garde Jazz," in *Uptown Conversation: The New Jazz Studies*, ed. Robert G. O'Meally, Brent Hayes Edwards, and Farah Jasmine Griffin (Columbia University Press, 2004), 34.

2. Charles S. Johnson, "Jazz Poetry and Blues," *The Carolina Magazine* 58, no. 7 (May 1928): 16–20.
3. Brent Hayes Edwards, *Epistrophies: Jazz and the Literary Imagination* (Harvard University Press, 2017), 12.
4. Duke University, "A Reading with Nathaniel Mackey with Bassist Vattell Cherry," YouTube, April 15, 2015, educational video, https://www.youtube.com/watch?v=r7UE1EguQVs&t=1382s.
5. Matana Roberts, "Mississippi Moonchile," YouTube, October 17, 2011, educational video, https://www.youtube.com/watch?v=JbNKUAyoQik.
6. "From a Reporter's Notebook," *Metronome* 75, no. 4 (April 1958), 42.
7. Ralph J. Gleason, "Perspectives," *Down Beat* 24, no. 23 (November 14, 1957), 20.
8. Nat Hentoff, "That Empty Jazz Fiction: Weary Blues, Part Two," *Metronome* 75, no. 3 (March 1958), 6.
9. Roy Toffler, "This Could Be the Start," letter to editor, *Down Beat* 24, no. 15 (July 25, 1957), 6.
10. Gleason, "Perspectives," 20.
11. All the music discussed in this essay is widely available on streaming services.
12. For examples that discuss improvisation in this way, see: Ingrid Monson, *Saying Something: Jazz Improvisation and Interaction* (University of Chicago Press, 1996); Paul F. Berliner, *Thinking in Jazz: The Infinite Art of Improvisation* (University of Chicago Press, 1994).
13. Of course, the hip cultural examples were not uniformly shallow. For a thoughtful consideration of the factors at play in this movement see: Phil Ford, *Dig: Sound and Music in Hip Culture* (Oxford University Press, 2013).
14. Rexroth, as quoted in Sascha Feinstein, *Jazz Poetry: From the 1920s to the Present* (Greenwood Press, 1997), 77.
15. Feinstein, *Jazz Poetry*, 78.
16. For an example, see: "The Beat Generation (Atlantic Advertisement)," *Jazz Today*, November 1957, 26.
17. Dom Cerulli, "The East," *Down Beat Music*, 1958.
18. Vilde Aaslid, "The Poetic Mingus and the Politics of Genre in String Quartet No. 1," *Journal of the Society for American Music* 9, no. 1 (February 2015): 1–25, https://doi.org/10.1017/S1752196314000522.
19. Jazz is certainly not unique in this regard. European classical music has had a historical fluctuation in the prevalence of the composer's role and the performer's role. Improvisation has, at times, been an important part of this musical tradition, both as a performance practice and a component of the compositional process. But, as John Howland puts it, "In classical music culture that was the legacy of Beethoven, the powerful romantic myth of

artistic genius has made it a virtual prerequisite that true musical art be entirely written and orchestrated by the composer." John Louis Howland, *Ellington Uptown: Duke Ellington, James P. Johnson, and the Birth of Concert Jazz* (University of Michigan Press, 2009), 263–64.

20. For a helpful introduction to these issues, see: Katherine Williams, "Improvisation as Composition: Fixity of Form and Collaborative Composition in Duke Ellington's *Diminuendo and Crescendo in Blue*," *Jazz Perspectives* 6, nos. 1–2: 223–46, https://doi.org/10.1080/17494060.2012.729712.
21. Nichole T. Rustin, "Mingus Fingers: Charles Mingus, Black Masculinity, and Postwar Jazz Culture" (PhD diss., New York University, 1999), 159.
22. For details about these appearances, see: Brigid Cohen, *Musical Migration and Imperial New York: Early Cold War Scenes*, New Material Histories of Music (University of Chicago Press, 2022), 65.
23. For an excellent analysis of these sessions, see chapter 1 of Cohen, *Musical Migration.*
24. George E. Lewis, "Improvised Music after 1950: Afrological and Eurological Perspectives," *Black Music Research Journal* 16, no. 1 (Spring 1996): 96.
25. Cohen, *Musical Migration*, 38–61.
26. Kevin McNeilly, "Charles Mingus Splits, or, All the Things You Could Be by Now If Sigmund Freud's Wife Was Your Mother," *Canadian Review of American Studies* 27, no. 2: 68.
27. Charles Mingus, liner notes to *Pithecanthropus Erectus,* Atlantic 1237, 1956.
28. Charles Hersch, "'Let Freedom Ring!': Free Jazz and African-American Politics," *Cultural Critique*, no. 32 (Winter 1995–1996): 97–123.
29. Jeff Schwartz, "New Black Music: Amiri Baraka (LeRoi Jones) and Jazz, 1959–1965" (PhD diss., Bowling Green State University, 2004).
30. For a helpful exploration of the role of notation in music, see: S. Andrew Granade, "Cracking the Code: What Notation Can Tell Us About Our Musical Values," *Open Access Musicology* 1 (2020): 1–29.
31. Mingus, *Pithecanthropus Erectus* notes.
32. Charles Mingus, Sue Mingus, and Andrew Homzy, *Charles Mingus, More than a Fake Book* (Jazz Workshop, 1991).
33. Scott Andrew Saul, *Freedom Is, Freedom Ain't: Jazz and the Making of the Sixties* (Harvard University Press, 2003), 162.
34. Mingus, as quoted in Nichole T. Rustin, "Cante Hondo: Charles Mingus, Nat Hentoff, and Jazz Racism," *Critical Sociology* 32, no. 2/3 (March 2006): 321.
35. The text of the piece is not, strictly speaking, poetry. But strict distinctions are not especially helpful here. Much of what the Beat poets were performing

was aimed at dismantling rigid distinctions between poetry and other kinds of language use, and the narration in Mingus's recordings falls very much in line with that practice despite not appearing strictly poetic in register.

36. Langston Hughes also contributed to the conceptualization of the narrative. For more information on Hughes's role, see Anthony Reed, *Soundworks: Race, Sound, and Poetry in Production* (Duke University Press, 2021), 80.
37. Reed, *Soundworks*, 81.
38. Brian Priestley, *Mingus: A Critical Biography* (Quartet Books, 1982), 89.
39. Stewart, as quoted in the liner notes to *A Modern Symposium of Music and Poetry,* Bethlehem, 1972.
40. The full text of the narration can be found here: Lexis, "Forgotten Treasure: Charles Mingus 'Scenes in the City' (1957)," Music Is My Sanctuary, October 17, 2015, https://www.musicismysanctuary.com/forgotten-treasure-charles-mingus-scenes-in-the-city-1957.
41. For some introduction to Mingus's famous autobiography, see: Thomas Carmichael, "*Beneath the Underdog*: Charles Mingus, Representation, and Jazz Autobiography," *Canadian Review of American Studies* 25, no. 3 (Fall 1995): 29–40; Nichole Rustin-Paschal, *The Kind of Man I Am: Jazzmasculinity and the World of Charles Mingus Jr.* (Wesleyan University Press, 2017).

CHAPTER THREE

MARATHI KIRTAN BEFORE AND AFTER "THE CLASSICAL"

Anna Christine Schultz

When ethnomusicologist/cultural historians Anna Morcom and Davesh Soneji invited me to join them on a panel called "Canon, Classification, and Indian Classical Performing Arts," I thought they had the wrong person. My research is on Indian devotional/popular music rather than classical music, but they got me thinking: why aren't the musics I study considered classical? So, I accepted the challenge and found clues in the fascinating Marathi biography of Govindbuva Hoshing, a performer of the genre known as naradiya kirtan. By approaching kirtan through the frame of this panel, I was able to nuance my earlier work on kirtan, bringing issues of caste and colonialism into sharper focus.

More broadly, I come to this research as a white American ethnomusicologist grappling with my discipline's colonial legacies. Trained in Euro-American classical music, I ask what a comparative treatment of the "classical" can teach us about the Orientalist bifurcation of the world into the "West" and the "Non-West." While this project is explicitly about caste, religion, and performance in

India, it is implicitly about a larger discursive frame in which the "classical" in Europe was constructed through colonial encounter as much as the "classical" in India was created within and against that encounter.

THE BOUNDARIES OF "THE CLASSICAL"

According to the *Harper Collins Dictionary of Music*, "classical music" is "a term sometimes used to distinguish serious or art music from popular and folk music. The distinction tends to be arbitrary, and the term itself is too vague to be useful."[1] Other studies of the "classical" in European music add historicizing nuance, noting the term's emergence in the eighteenth century, and further elaboration in the nineteenth century, to denote high-status music, a "golden age" canon of composers and compositions, transcendence, and seriousness.[2] What these myriad meanings share is an eye toward boundaries—of class (high vs. low), time (the ideal past vs. unruly present), authorship (anonymous orality vs. written composition), and rigor (serious vs. light or popular). You may notice that each binary is organized hierarchically, with classical music falling on the winning side.

I begin this India-focused article with Western classical music not in search a universal definition but, rather, because histories of the "classical" in India and in Europe are inextricably entwined. Even as "classical music" in Europe was erected in opposition to stylistic, class, and cultural "others," Indian scholars, nationalists, and musicians were using the English concept of "classical music" and its Sanskritic translation, "*shastriya sangeet*," to erect boundaries of their own. As Amanda Weidman argues,

> Western classical music was not a fully formed entity that was merely exported to India beginning in the early twentieth century; rather, ideas about classical music, both Western and Indian, were being negotiated simultaneously in the colony and the metropole.[3]

Charles Burney and John Hawkins, music historians active in the early construction of "classical music" in Europe, were in dialogue with Sir William Jones (1746–1794), a British Orientalist[4] and author of the first English-language book on Indian music that in turn shaped nineteenth-century Indian music histories by Indian and British scholars.[5]

Hindustani music emerged in North Indian, mostly Muslim courts between the sixteenth and nineteenth centuries and was "rebranded" as "classical" during the height of cultural nationalism in the late-nineteenth and early twentieth centuries.[6] Before the era of classical reform led by high-caste (mostly Brahmin) Hindu musicologists and musicians, Hindustani music was learned aurally through a system of discipleship with esteemed teacher-artists, most of whom were Muslim. Music societies like the Poona Gayan Samaj and Brahmin musicologists like S. M. Tagore and V. N. Bhatkhande sought to mold this music into a national classical form that was at once modern and rooted in a Hindu past. To do this they took a page from the Orientalist book, positioning modern Hindustani performance in a lineage with ancient Sanskrit texts (*shastras*), lending it the gravitas of antiquity while attempting to cover the tracks of its largely Islamicate origins.[7] Indeed, a more literal translation of "shastriya" ("classical") is "relating to the scriptures,"[8] and it is important to note that Sanskrit is often restricted to Brahman or other high-caste men.[9] They also sought to systematize and modernize performance practice, concert culture, and education. Put succinctly, for classicizing musicologists and musicians, reform was necessary to make music worthy of the national stage.[10] They drew on a discourse of boundaries born of colonial modernity to shore up social power and articulate (Hindu) national identity. While they succeeded in making Hindustani music classical, their efforts at Hinduization, modernization, and pedagogical reform were only partial. It remains a messy, contested terrain in which Hindus, Muslims, and others participate, and in which older pedagogical methods are nurtured alongside the new.[11]

For many in South Asia, as in Europe, classical music is not just a context or concept, but also a sound. You know it when you hear it. North Indian classical music is based on melodic/modal frameworks known as *raga* and rhythmic cycles known as *tala*; songs and compositions realized in performance through often virtuosic improvisation; and an extensive repertory of genre- and instrument-specific practices of ornamentation. This vocal performance by Manali Bose offers an eloquent glimpse of Hindustani musical aesthetics: the slow, delicate unfolding of the raga (the pentatonic *kalavati*), accompanied by the sixteen-beat *tintal* played by the *tabla* (a drum in two parts played with fingers and hands), in which she explores the shades of meaning in the text through increasingly virtuosic, genre-specific bends, ornaments, and runs.[12] But *is* the classical always audible? This simple question requires a more complicated answer. Several North Indian genres share the modes, meters, and improvisation techniques of Hindustani music, but are excluded from the classical canon or are marked as "light" and thus "less classical." Anna Morcom refers to the "cultures of exclusion" that have kept the bodies and styles of North Indian hereditary female performers out of the classical traditions despite their obvious contributions to its genesis.[13] Davesh Soneji's forthcoming monograph draws our attention to similar occlusions in South India, namely of Muslim musicians and compositions whose raga music is excluded from the classical canon despite its audible similarity to the styles deemed "classical."[14] Although the concept of the classical may be "too vague to be *useful*," it has nonetheless been *used* to separate and stigmatize groups of people.

It might be more productive, then, to speak of classicization as a (boundary-making) process rather than "the classical" as a set of musical attributes. Classicization is shaped by the same paradox as nationalism and Orientalism and is imbricated with both: it is a distinctly modern practice that presumes and idealizes antiquity, marginalizing sounds and practices that fall outside its arbitrary boundaries. Historian Partha Chatterjee writes of the "classicization of tradition,"

> A nation, or so at least the nationalist believes, must have a past. If nineteenth-century Englishmen could claim, with scant regard for the particularities of geography or anthropology, a cultural ancestry in classical Greece, there was no reason why nineteenth-century Bengalis could not

> claim one in the Vedic age. All that was necessary was a classicization of tradition. [...] A classicization of tradition was, in any case, a prior requirement for the vertical appropriation of sanitized popular traditions.[15]

In this article, I argue that some music, paradoxically, benefits socially from sounding classical while vigorously resisting classicization. Given the colonial, nationalist, middle-class belief in classicization as betterment, why might some people reject classicization? I explore this question in relation to *naradiya kirtan*, a sacred song/narrative genre from Marathi-speaking western India. Through this study of the boundary between North Indian classical music and Marathi naradiya kirtan—blurry in the 19th century and reified in the 20th—I hope to offer new perspectives on place, caste, piety, and classicization.

NARADIYA KIRTAN AT THE BOUNDARY OF THE CLASSICAL

In the mid-nineteenth century, naradiya kirtan was performed in temples by a Brahmin singer/storyteller, known as a *kirtankar*, accompanied by a small ensemble that would include two or more of the following: a plucked drone (*tambura*[16] or *veena*[17]), a drum (*pakhawaj*[18] or *tabla*[19]), *sarangi*[20] (a resonant bowed lute), and small hand cymbals (*jhanjh*[21]) played by the kirtankar himself. It was primarily presentational and solo, with the audience joining in only for certain chants and devotional songs. It was also eclectic, drawing on a wide range of Hindustani genres like *khayal*, *dhrupad*, and *thumri*, and an even larger collection of Marathi genres, like *abhanga*, *shloka*, *arya*, *saki*, *dindi*, *ovi*, and so forth. The audible similarities between Hindustani music and naradiya kirtan are significant. Not only did kirtankars draw on Hindustani genres; they also used Hindustani raga, tala, and khayal-inflected virtuosity, and they moved through an improvisation in a way that mirrored Hindustani practice. This performance of an invocatory kirtan song (*naman*) by Dattadas Ghag is a good indication of just how classical some naradiya kirtankars sound, even today.[22] Listen to how he traverses the same raga (kalavati) as Manali Bose, returning to repetitions of "Jayjay Ram Krishna Hari" (Praise to Ram Krishna Vishnu) after improvisations that become higher and increasingly virtuosic over time, always retaining the melodic flexibility and ornamental practices of Hindustani music.

Much research on the classicization of Hindustani music focuses on how it marginalized and erased hereditary musicians, but this article explores classicization from a different vantage point. It is about Brahmin naradiya kirtankars who absorbed techniques from Hindustani music while *rejecting* Hindustani music as too Islamic and insufficiently pious. I agree with Jaime Jones, who writes, "There is no such thing as 'sacred music' in South Asia, but one might argue that all South Asian music is potentially sacred."[23] In rejecting Indian classical music, kirtankars drew a boundary not only between Hindus and Muslims, but also—somewhat arbitrarily—between orientations that might be considered "sacred" and "secular." This boundary has only deepened with time, and in the current post-classicization era, consumers readily identify genres like *bhajan,* kirtan, and *qawwali* as "devotional" and other genres, like khayal, *kriti,* and dhrupad[24] as "classical."[25]

In this article, I turn toward a narrative about naradiya kirtan's emergence, a time when kirtankars drew liberally on Hindustani raga and North Indian vocal genres, and Marathi kirtankars trod some of the same territory as court musicians.[26] Some, including the father of famed classical singer, reformer, and nationalist V. D. Paluskar, were supported by the rulers of small princely states.[27] At these courts they encountered singers trained in North Indian khayal (the dominant genre of Hindustani vocal music since the nineteenth century) before khayal had become classical. My discussion centers on one such kirtankar, Govindbuva Hoshing Nashikkar (1814–1888; see Figure 3.1) and my main source is his 1925 Marathi biography by Ramkrishnabuva Dhole, *Pūrvāśramī Govindbuvā Hośiṅg Nāśikkar Yāñce Caritra* (*Biography of the Late Govindbuva Hoshing Nashikkar*; see Figure 3.2).[28]

Figure 3.1. Govindbuva Hoshing, as pictured in his 1925 biography by Ramkrishnabuva Dhole.

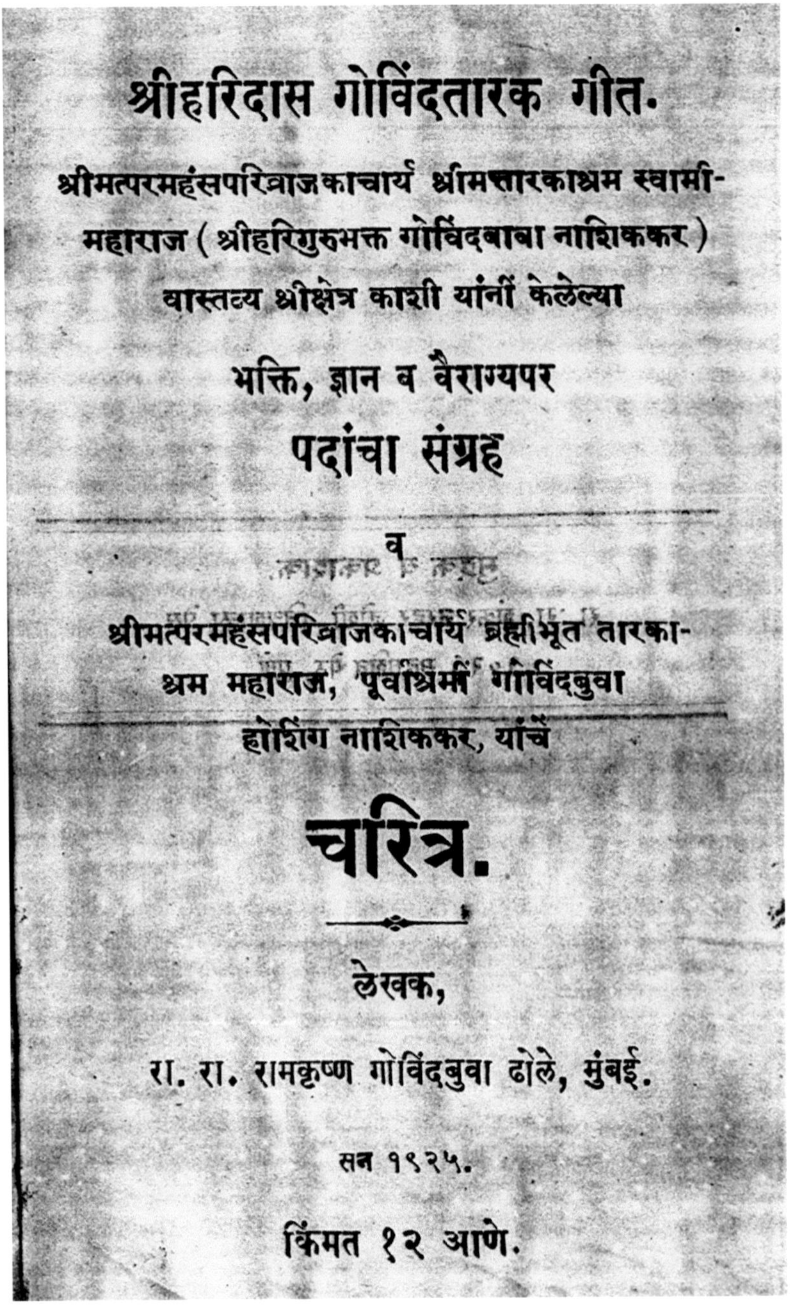

श्रीहरिदास गोविंदतारक गीत.

श्रीमत्परमहंसपरिव्राजकाचार्य श्रीमत्तारकाश्रम स्वामी-
महाराज (श्रीहरिगुरुभक्त गोविंदबावा नाशिककर)
वास्तव्य श्रीक्षेत्र काशी यांनीं केलेल्या

भक्ति, ज्ञान व वैराग्यपर

पदांचा संग्रह

व

श्रीमत्परमहंसपरिव्राजकाचार्य ब्रह्मीभूत तारका-
श्रम महाराज, पूर्वाश्रमीं गोविंदबुवा
होशिंग नाशिककर, यांचें

चरित्र.

लेखक,

रा. रा. रामकृष्ण गोविंदबुवा ढोले, मुंबई.

सन १९२५.

किंमत १२ आणे.

Figure 3.2. Cover of Ramkrishnabuva Dhole, *Śrīharidāsa Govindatāraka Gīta va Pūrvāśramī Govindbuvā Hośiṅg Nāśikkar Yāñce Caritra* [Shriharidasa Govindatāraka Songs and Biography of the Late Govindbuva Hoshing Nashikkar] (Citrashāḷā Press, 1925).

Hoshing performed kirtan before the emergence of the modern classical traditions, but his biography was written after the "classical" was firmly established within the Indian national imaginary.[29] Naradiya kirtankars today consider Hoshing to be the originator of naradiya kirtan, with its unique form, repertoire of genres, style of performance, and caste composition. Most naradiya kirtankars, like Hoshing, are Brahmins, while performers of *varkari kirtan*, the other main style of Marathi kirtan, are drawn from all castes. Among other innovations, kirtankars today credit Hoshing with innovating the two-part form of naradiya kirtan, wherein the first half, called *purvaranga,* is a religious discourse on a topic like devotion, guru (spiritual teacher), service, and so on, and the second half, the *uttararanga,* is a story illustrating that topic.[30]

Hoshing's biographer, Ramkrishna Dhole, was himself a well-known kirtankar and the son of one of Hoshing's disciples. Dhole was active in the 1910s and '20s, when cultural nationalism had become firmly aligned with an explicitly anticolonial political agenda, and kirtankars were rubbing elbows with Lokmanya Tilak, a Maharashtrian Brahmin and nationalist leader. Both Tilak and Dhole were active in the All-India Kirtan Conference, held annually between 1917 and 1922, with Tilak acting as president in 1918 and Dhole serving as a member of the welcoming committee in 1920. Much as with Hindustani music, kirtankars participating in the conferences sought to modernize and systematize kirtan to make it interesting for educated listeners.[31] But they also saw this as a mission to return kirtan to its previous glory following disruption by British colonizers. Laying bare this nationalist agenda, conference president Krishnapantji Khadilkar told kirtankars at the 1921 conference that "since there is Hindustani and Karnataki music, one should also try to develop a Maharashtrian type of music,"[32] a sentiment that resonates through Dhole's biography. Govind Sakharam Sardesai, in his introduction to Dhole's biography of Hoshing, wrote, "Though western knowledge of today is contaminating our national life, changing it dramatically, a biography like this is very useful for awakening society to the memory of old religious and moral traditions, and of an institution that was preserved."[33] In that vein, Dhole idealizes nineteenth-century kirtan. His fascination for that era's fluid boundaries between classical genres like khayal, devotional genres like kirtan, and stage genres like *natya sangit*, is balanced by a newer, nationalist, classicizing investment in boundaries of caste, religion, and place. In Dhole's account, Hoshing goes to the same spaces, receives the same gifts, and sings the same songs as traditional Muslim musicians specializing in khayal, but socially and religiously, he is a world apart. Soon after reformists had classicized Hindustani music, Dhole's kirtan biography reimagines an Indian nation that is more Hindu, more Marathi, and more Brahmin than that of classicizing musicologists. Dhole's account is as much hagiography as it is secular biography—every biographical episode has a touch of the miraculous, with Hoshing demonstrating superhuman musical skills alongside unmatched spiritual superiority.[34]

A MARATHI NARADIYA KIRTANKAR IN NORTH INDIA

Dhole's biography of Hoshing begins in the Maharashtrian town of Nashik and ends in the North Indian pilgrimage center of Varanasi (also known as Kashi). The biography's expansive geography demonstrates what Adheesh Sathaye refers to, in relation to narratives of the sage Viswamitra, as "geo-mapping the Brahmin Other," a grounding of scriptural stories in present-day sites, which serves "1) to extend Brahminical authority onto pilgrimage sites across the subcontinent and (2) to construct new, regionalized inflections of Brahmin social power."[35] Throughout Hoshing's journey, from his birth in Nashik to his death in Kashi, each place of political power is paired with a holy site, rendering his journey part performance tour and part pilgrimage. As Hoshing ventured northward to increasingly distant locales, he became more and more engaged in court performance while marking his difference from court performers. Figure 3.3 illustrates this journey, which begins in Nashik and Trimbakeshwar, then moves to Bombay, Pune, Khandesh, Indore, Dwarka, Baroda, and finally, Lashkar, Gwalior, and Varanasi, in that order. The points proceed according to the colors of the rainbow, with red as Hoshing's starting place in and around Nashik, and purple being his final resting place in

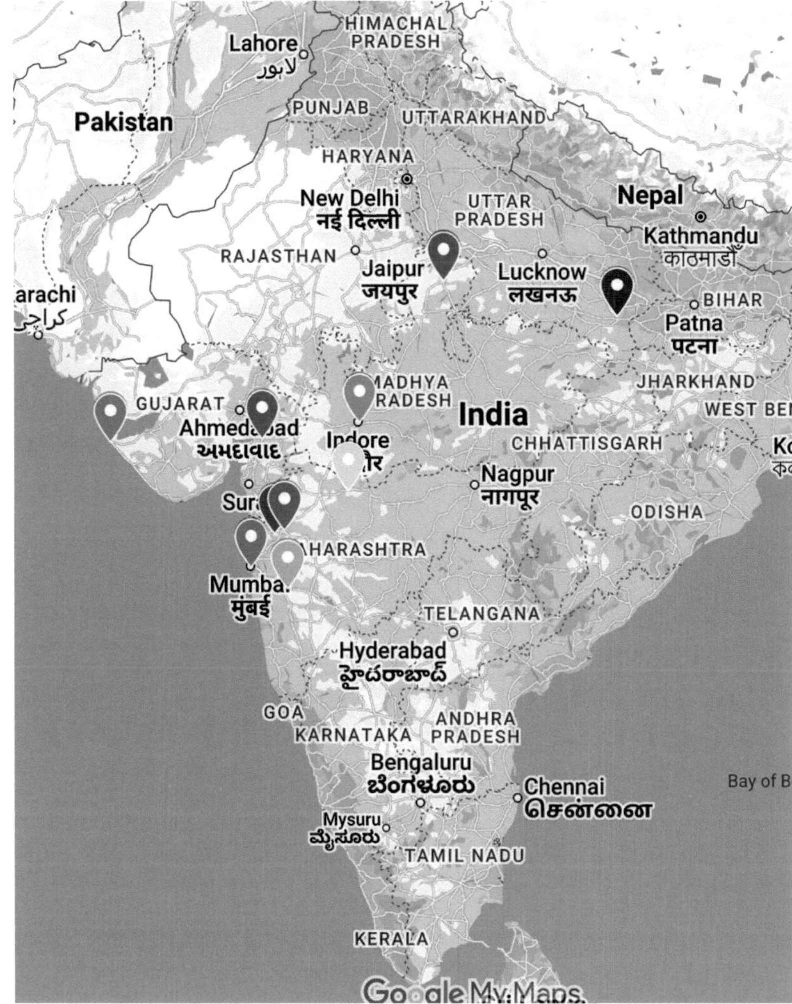

Figure 3.3. Map of places where Hoshing performed or lived.

Kashi. In Dhole's account, however, Hoshing's court-sponsored appearances were peripheral to his sacred grounding. Not only does Hoshing's expansive journey underscore his spiritual emplacement; it also covers much of the same ground, literally, as Hindustani music, a diverse region of Marathi, Gujarati, and Hindi speakers encompassed by a singular classical tradition.

Govindbuva Hoshing's father was from Trimbakeshwar, home to one of India's twelve sacred *Jyotirlinga*[36] sites, but he moved to nearby Nashik—which was both city and pilgrimage site—for greater opportunities as a kirtankar.[37] Govindbuva (b. 1814)[38] followed in his father's footsteps, honing his craft as a kirtankar in and around Nashik, but it was on trips to Pune and Mumbai that he proved he could measure up to—and indeed exceed—the skill of other kirtankars. Dhole portrayed Pune as a hub for North Indian vocal music and as a home for naradiya kirtan, a reputation that it retains until today. It was in Pune that someone suggested his kirtans might be even more appealing if he infused them with dhrupad and *dhamar* (today, considered "heavy" classical vocal genres), so he lived with music teacher Sakharambowa Kashikar of the famed *gharana*[39] (or musical house) of Gwalior until he had learned one hundred and twenty-five dhrupad compositions. Armed with these new musical skills, the next time he came to Pune to perform kirtan, he outperformed even the most skilled Gwalior gharana-trained kirtankars.[40]

In one story from the Pune chapter, Dhole describes how Hoshing stood to perform kirtan in the famous eighteenth-century Tulshibaug Rama Temple, only to be sonically attacked by a rival. He writes:

> As Govindbuva's fame began to grow, so did Trimbakarajabuva's jealousy...
>
> Later, Trimbakrajbuva devised a new strategy to harass him. At the time, there was an excellent pakhawaj[[41]] player in Pune named Balakrishna Manyaba Koditkar. [Trimbakrajbuva] offered him ten rupees and said, "Tonight, halfway through the performance, break your drum and spoil the event to disgrace Shri Govindbuva." He agreed to this. Shri Govindbuva's kirtan started at nine pm in Tulshibaug. The audience was huge that day. There was barely enough room for *Buva* [an honorific for naradiya kirtankars] to stand; the rest of the temple was packed all the way to the door. After performing the purvaranga for about an hour, Shrigovindbuva sang a dhrupad while *buka* [a black powder] was

applied to listeners' foreheads. Four men circulated through the temple with buka plates, but even still, there were so many people that it took a whole hour to apply buka... On the final "dha" of the dhrupad, Koditkar struck the drum and broke it. Buva understood what had happened. If Shri Govindbuva had informed anyone about this, ten drums and the same number of players would have appeared instantly. But instead, he chanted "*Sitakant smarana jayjay Ram*"[[42]] loudly and began telling his uttararanga story on the death of Abhimanyu [a warrior of the Mahabharata epic]. First, he conveyed heroism (*vir rasa*) with an intensity that thrilled listeners; they were so excited that they felt ready to take up arms and go to battle. And after that he expressed pathos (*karuna rasa*) so convincingly that the audience was moved to tears and began sobbing. Govindbuva did all this without singing any songs, so neither small cymbals[[43]] nor pakhawaj were needed. His accompanists just stood playing tambura[[44]] all night long.[[45]] First there was bravery, then love, then pathos, and finally humor. Finally, he narrated the episode of Jayadratha's slaying [and the kirtan was over]... Feeling the presence of the divine, the audience showered Shri Govindbuva with flowers. Then Buva said that Manyaba Koditkar was the reason for the vibrancy of today's story. With these words, he draped a gold-bordered shawl worth two hundred rupees over Manyaba. Hearing this, Manyaba repented and began to cry; he put his head on Shri Govindbuva's feet and said, "I made a mistake; please forgive me."[46]

After affirming Govindbuva Hoshing's expertise as a dhrupad singer, Dhole recounts the artist's split-second decision to perform an entire uttararanga without song. Uttararangas consist of spoken storytelling interspersed with songs that enhance the story's emotional impact, so Dhole's hagiography communicates that Hoshing had a near-miraculous ability to enthrall audiences using only his speaking voice. This theme is found throughout the biography: that Hoshing's musical skills exceeded those of Hindustani musicians, but that his *real* superpower was an ability to communicate his vast (Brahminical) religious knowledge. His spiritual superiority was clinched by concluding the kirtan with a generous gift to a man who tried to undermine him. In so doing, he won a public match *and* his rival's emissary's devotion.

If this success in Pune marks the beginning of Hoshing's career, his migration to Varanasi signifies its culmination.[47] During the mid-nineteenth century, Varanasi—known throughout the biography by its Vedic name of Kashi—was the site of a vibrant thumri (a genre of romantic, poetry-centric vocal music, often considered "light") and khayal vocal music scene dominated by hereditary women performers of the Benares gharana, but there is no mention of that. Instead, Kashi is where Hoshing performs kirtan amid an austere regime of Sanskrit scripture study and Brahminical daily ritual.[48]

> Maharaj[[49]] woke up at four in the morning, bathed in the Ganges, did early morning prayers, and went home. Then he did *bhagwatpujan*,[[50]] read twelve chapters of the *Shrimad Bhagwat*,[[51]] then took *darshan*[[52]] of Shri Vishweshwar, took a ritual bath in the Manakirnaka,[[53]] recited midday prayers,[[54]] made water offerings,[[55]] and went back home at twelve to serve everyone a meal. Then he took a bit of rest and began his kirtan right at three, concluding it exactly when it was time for evening prayers.[[56]] Then he did his evening prayers at the Ganges and for three hours at night walked and sang *bhajans* [devotional songs] in Pandharpur[[57]] tunes. Then he went to sleep. This is what he did for the entire *chaturmas*.[58]

This superhuman schedule renders kirtan but a small slice out of a busy day of religious study and ritual observance during the holy months of *chaturmas*, ending his day with a Pandharpur tune from a Marathi pilgrimage town, a reminder that he was not just a Brahmin, but a specifically *Maharashtrian* Brahmin.

Having established the bodily Brahmin piety of Hoshing's life in Varanasi, Dhole then positioned him as a visitor in the world of North Indian court performance and khayal-based raga. The next chapter of *Biography of the Late Govindbuva Hoshing Nashikkar,* set in Lashkar,

Figure 3.4. Shrimant Jayajirao Shinde, Photo by Talboys Wheeler from "The Imperial Assemblage," 1877.

Figure 3.5. Jayajirao Shinde's Darbar, photograph of mural, 1905.

Gwalior, narrates how Shrimant Jayajirao Shinde (see Figure 3.4), a music-, art-, and liquor-loving Hindu Maratha ruler of the princely Gwalior state under British colonial rule, became his devotee and patron.[59] The Shindes had been ruling first Ujjain and then Gwalior since the early eighteenth century, in Dhole's account becoming northernized and Islamicate during their multigenerational northern sojourn.[60] Indeed, Jayajirao was the patron of Haddu and Hassu Khan, founders of the Gwalior gharana, which is widely considered to be the first gharana of Hindustani music.[61]

Hoshing's first performance in Lashkar hosted by Shinde Sarkar (King Shinde) was a lavish affair attended by a coterie of important political leaders; women listening from behind a curtain; Brahmin scholars; khayal artists Haddu Khan, Hassu Khan, and Nathu Khan; and famed sitarists Miyataheb and Amir Khan, among other "various Muslims." The tent was arranged in the manner of Shinde's court (see Figure 3.5 for a painting of his court) and included a throne that would allow the king to sit comfortably. When Govindbuva stood to perform kirtan, flanked by his vocal and instrumental accompanists, there was an expanse of about fifteen thousand people outside the tent. As he began singing a devotional song in Raga Yaman, a hush fell over the crowd. Dhole narrates how the great khayal vocalist, Haddu Khan exclaimed:

> "*Wa!*[62] Govindbuva, wa! You are God!"[63] and bowed down to him in a *salaam*,[64] which those gathered were fortunate to see… After the introductory songs, he performed "*Balakrishna charani laksha lago*"[65] [May I behold Lord Krishna's feet], sang a devotional hymn to Krishna, then loudly called out, "*Pundalika varde hari Vitthala*" [Hari Vitthala, grant blessings to Pundalika], with the chanting of the audience echoing in the sky."[66]

Then Govind Maharaj began the spoken portion of his kirtan by gesturing toward Shrimant Sarkar and saying that the council of rulers exceeds even Indra's divine assembly. Having thus honored the king, he explained that each person listens to kirtan according to their own ability and that for the sarkar to enjoy the kirtan, he needed his mace-bearer to announce his entry with great pomp, and his courtiers to bring him a hookah and cigarettes. The sarkar was ashamed of his vanity, vowed to submit to any of Govindbuva's orders, and ordered his courtiers to sit quietly during the kirtan. The sarkar was dazzled by the knowledge, oratory, and sweetness of Govindbuva's performance. By the end of the kirtan he referred to him as "*Ishwar*" [God] and by the end of the week, had become his disciple.[67]

This episode depicts the crowning victory in Dhole's account of what we might call Hoshing's northern campaign. He wins the devotion of a powerful northern patron while ushering the king back to the Marathi Hindu fold. Moreover, he beats legendary Muslim musicians of the Gwalior khayal gharana at their own game, all while maintaining a rigorous schedule of Brahminical observance. This narrative, written *after* the formation of the classical about a time *before* the classical, reverses the geography of musical diffusion. In the more common classical history narrative, Balkrishnabuva Ichalakaranjikar (1849–1926), a Maharashtrian vocalist, traveled from Maharashtra to Gwalior to learn khayal and then brought his new knowledge back to Maharashtra, where it took root and became a central factor in the making of the (Hindustani) classical.[68] Instead of northern music traveling to Maharashtra, here Maharashtrian music—kirtan—goes north, absorbing khayal as it does almost any genre. This process, which we might call Brahmin sonic colonialism, is enabled through the eclecticism of naradiya kirtan's form, in which an improvisation in Raga Yaman is heard next to Hoshing's signature devotional tune, "Balkrishna Charani Laksha Lago"[69] and the traditional Marathi kirtan chant, "Pundalika Varda Hari Vitthala." In this old recording, former kirtankar Ramchandrabuva Karhadkar, who belongs to Hoshing's performance lineage, sang a version of Hoshing's "Balakrishna Charani Laksha Lago," replacing "Balakrishna" with "Sitarama."[70]

This hagiography could not be told in this way if it were not for the geographic imaginaries born of colonialism that tether castes and religious communities to specific regions. In Dhole's account, part of what is so remarkable about Hoshing's story is just how far from Maharashtra he traveled without ever losing his Marathiness. Hoshing was not, however, the first Marathi Brahmin to move north and become adept at North Indian court music; indeed, Justin Scarimbolo's masterful dissertation discusses just that: the Marathi Brahmin Ashtewale family who became patrons and disciples of North Indian khayal musicians in Ujjain in 1818.[71] What is different about Hoshing's story as told by Dhole is that classical music is subordinated to and engulfed by kirtan.

The ritual context of kirtan, in which listeners make offerings rather than payment, and the sarkar is a devotee/disciple rather than a patron, also allows Dhole to narrate a story of a well-compensated artist unencumbered by the stigma of professional musicianship. Today, kirtan offerings come from individual listeners in the form of small amounts of money placed on the arti plate, or sometimes as rice or other gifts placed at the kirtankar's shawl after a performance (see Figure 3.6). They may

Figure 3.6. Arti during a naradiya kirtan by H. Bh. P. Sadananda Gokhale at the Akhil Bharatiya Kirtan Sanstha (All-India Kirtan Society), Mumbai, 2015.

also come in the form of a check offered—also on the arti plate—by a hosting organization or patron. In the nineteenth century, many kirtankars were employed at the courts of landowners and kings. As we saw in the last story, though, the king is framed not as a patron, but as a devotee. Hoshing teaches Shinde Sarkar to maintain the sanctity of the temple, keeping him from transforming it into a court. The king responds by subordinating himself as Hoshing's disciple.

This sacred economy of offerings notwithstanding, Dhole details the gifts that Hoshing received from rulers and landowners: in Nashik, a garland of five thousand pearls from the prime minister, Govindrao Rode; in Mumbai, five-hundred-rupee earrings, a string of pearls around his neck, a gold bracelet on his wrist, seven long turban cloths in seven colors, silk dhotis to wear, and shawls embroidered with silver thread; in Lashkar, a fifty-thousand-rupee string of pearls from Hinduraaybaba; and from the Shinde Sarkar, one hundred thousand rupees to build a temple on the banks of the Ganges in Kashi, and a large hermitage with an idol that cost four thousand rupees.[72]

According to Dhole's account, Hoshing lived comfortably, but gave away many of the glamorous gifts he received. He wore the silk clothes from Mumbai only once before giving them to needy people, he made requests of Shinde Sarkar that were not material in nature, and he demanded that the sarkar pay other kirtankars handsomely.[73] In sum, Dhole demonstrated that Hoshing possessed the selfless detachment from worldly reward befitting a spiritual leader, while also measuring his success in sumptuous material terms.

Govindbuva Hoshing was an exceptional figure in terms of skill and ambition, but he was not the only kirtankar to attract the attention of royal patrons in the nineteenth century and earlier. Peshwa Bajirao II, who ruled the Maratha empire from 1795 to 1818, appointed Antaji Manakeshwar as court kirtankar; Ramchandrabuva Kashikar was favored by various princes and traveled as far as the court of Nepal to perform; and Shridharshastri Deshpande was patronized by princes of Tanjore and Nepal. In each of those cases, the kirtankars were paid handsomely in gold, gems, money, and jewelry.[74]

More than for his success and skill as a kirtankar, Hoshing is remembered today for his lasting impact on the style and form of naradiya kirtan. First, he created the now de rigueur separation of naradiya kirtan into the purvaranga and uttararanga. Second, his compositions, such as "Balakrishna Charani Laksha Lago," continue to thrill kirtan audiences. Third, his influence extends beyond kirtan into Marathi musical theater (*sangit natak*). In 1887, just one year before Hoshing's death, the Kirloskar Natak Mandali (Kirloskar Drama Troupe), an important group in the early development of sangit natak, came to Kashi to hear him, and were—according to Dhole—deeply moved by his singing.[75] The lines between sangit natak and kirtan were blurry throughout the nineteenth and twentieth centuries, with several artists moving between the two performance contexts of stage and temple.[76]

CONCLUSION

Given all of this—the lavish compensation, the patronage of a powerful king, the liberal use of Hindustani raga, improvisation, and genres, and the ability to impress the most accomplished khayal artists—why did naradiya kirtan not become a classical art? From the point of view of kirtankars, this would have implied secularization and a loss of Brahmin prestige. Both Hindustani music and naradiya kirtan are gentrifying forces: Hindustani music by appropriating and reshaping the arts of hereditary performers; kirtan as a meta-genre that subsumes diverse genres like dhrupad, khayal, and thumri, and a panoply of Marathi devotional song genres.[77] Govindbuva Hoshing lived at a time when the boundaries of the classical had not yet been established, when court performance was a heteroreligious sphere. In transforming that history into nationalist memory, Dhole acknowledges the nineteenth century's overlapping musical spheres while framing them in Hindu–Muslim communalist[78] terms that became possible only *after* the classical. For the most conservative among Marathi Brahmins in the early twentieth century, it was not enough to appropriate the music of hereditary court and salon musicians and recontextualize it for concert settings. Instead, they embedded Hindustani music within the Brahmin ritual performance of naradiya kirtan. This rendered naradiya kirtan an arguably even *more* decisive tool than Brahminized classical music in maintaining Brahmin caste hegemony.

It is worth remembering that Ramkrishnabuva Dhole was a kirtankar writing about a kirtankar. Having heard the cadences of storytelling in innumerable Marathi kirtans, I can picture Dhole standing at the front of a temple, gesturing over the space to conjure an image of Hoshing similarly standing in front of a congregation seventy years prior. Indeed, a common device used by kirtankars today is to embed a story of a saint performing kirtan within one's own kirtan. As in the stories of saints told in a kirtan's uttararanga, Dhole recounts Hoshing's near-divine moral compass. With that compass as a guide, Hoshing charted a national space, rewriting classical music as sacred, Hindu, and Brahmin. Then, as now, the nation was contested—would it be secular and inclusive, or would it be Hindu, marginalizing religious minorities and oppressed castes? The Hindu nationalist surge that has only increased since the 1990s reminds us just how fragile secularism can be.

ACKNOWLEDGMENTS

I am grateful to Anna Morcom and Davesh Soneji for inviting me to develop this project for a session on "Canon, classification, and Indian performing arts" at the 2021 Annual Meeting of the Society for Ethnomusicology, and to Amanda Weidman for serving as our respondent. Thanks also to Joanna Bosse, Chris Scales, and Michael Largey for their feedback on a later version that I presented at Michigan State University.

NOTES

1. Christine Ammer, "Classical Music," in *The HarperCollins Dictionary of Music*, 3rd ed. (Harper Perennial, 1995), 85.
2. Matthew Gelbart, *The Invention of 'Folk Music' and 'Art Music': Emerging Categories from Ossian to Wagner* (Cambridge University Press, 2007); Lydia Goehr, *The Imaginary Museum of Musical Works: An Essay in the Philosophy of Music* (Oxford University Press, 1992), 247, as cited in Amanda Weidman, *Singing the Classical, Voicing the Modern: The Postcolonial Politcs of Music in South India* (Duke University Press, 2006), 5; Daniel Heartz and Bruce Alan Brown, "Classical," *Grove Music Online*, January 20, 2001, https://www.oxfordmusiconline.com/grovemusic/display/10.1093/gmo/9781561592630.001.0001/omo-9781561592630-e-0000005889; Virinder S. Kalra, *Sacred and Secular Musics: A Postcolonial Approach* (Bloomsbury, 2015), 43–65; William Weber, "The Contemporaneity of Eighteenth-Century Musical Tastes," *Musical Quarterly* 70, no. 2 (1984), 185.
3. Weidman, *Singing the Classical*, 288.
4. The term "orientalist" was used from the late eighteenth through early twentieth centuries to refer to European and American academics who researched and wrote about "the Orient," which was understood to include Asian and Middle Eastern societies. Edward Said argues that "Orientalism" is also a discourse that draws a clear boundary between "the East" and the "the West," stereotyping and essentializing the latter to serve the imperial power of the

latter. Edward Said, *Orientalism*, 25th Anniversary Edition (Vintage Books, 2003), 1–4.

5. Jaime Jones, "Music, History, and the Sacred in South Asia," in *The Cambridge History of World Music* (Cambridge University Press, 2013), 205–207; Kalra, *Sacred and Secular Musics*, 49–53; Lakshmi Subramanian, *From the Tanjore Court to the Madras Music Academy: A Social History of Music in South India* (OUP India, 2006), 56–72.
6. Max Katz, *Lineage of Loss: Counternarratives of North Indian Music* (Wesleyan University Press, 2017), 21; Harold S. Powers and Jonathan Katz, "India, §II: History of Classical Music," *Grove Music Online*, January 31, 2020, https://www.oxfordmusiconline.com/grovemusic/display/10.1093/gmo/9781561592630.001.0001/omo-9781561592630-e-0000043272#omo-9781561592630-e-0000043272-divi-0000043272.2; Ashok Da. Ranade, *Hindustani Music* (National Book Trust, 1997), 14–28.
7. Pandit Vishnu Narayan Bhatkhande, *Hindustani Sangitpaddhati, Bhag Pahila* (Popular Prakashan, 1992); Charles Capwell, "Representing 'Hindu' Music to the Colonial and Native Elite of Calcutta," in *Hindustani Music: Thirteenth to Twentieth Centuries*, ed. Joep Bor, Françoise 'Nalini' Delvoye, Jane Harvey, and Emmie te Nijenhuis (Manohar, 2010), 285–311, especially 297; Kalra, *Sacred and Secular Musics*, 46; Arvind-Pal S. Mandair, *Religion and the Specter of the West: Sikhism, India, Postcoloniality, and the Politics of Transition* (Columbia University Press, 2009), 61; Aneesh Pradhan, *Hindustani Music in Colonial Bombay* (Three Essays Collective, 2014), 68–71, 77–86. As Janaki Bakhle notes, Bhatkhande saw Hindustani music as having a Hindu past and future, but that it was not an unbroken tradition. Janaki Bakhle, *Two Men and Music: Nationalism in the Making of an Indian Classical Tradition* (Oxford University Press, 2005), 114–117.
8. J. T. Molesworth, *A Dictionary, Marathi and English*, Digital Dictionaries of South Asia, University of Chicago, accessed November 21, 2023, https://dsal.uchicago.edu/cgi-bin/app/molesworth_query.py?qs=शास्त्रीय&sear chhws=yes.
9. Anne Keßler-Persaud, "Sanskrit Texts and Language," *Brill's Encyclopedia of Hinduism Online*, ed. K. A. Jacobsen (Brill, 2018), https://doi.org/10.1163/2212-5019_BEH_COM_2010010.
10. Bakhle, *Two Men and Music*, 96–214; Joep Bor and Allyn Miner, "Hindustani Music: A Historical Overview of the Modern Period," in *Hindustani Music*, ed. Bor et al., 197–220; Anna Morcom, *Illicit Worlds of Indian Dance: Cultures of Exclusion* (Oxford University Press, 2013); Pradhan, *Hindustani Music in Colonial Bombay*; Regula Qureshi, "Whose Music? Sources and Contexts in Indic Musicology," in *Comparative Musicology and the Anthropology of Music*,

ed. Bruno Nettl and Philip V. Bohlman (University of Chicago Press, 1991), 152–168; Michael David Rosse, "Music Schools and Societies in Bombay c. 1864–1937," in *Hindustani Music*, ed. Bor et al., 313–330; David Trasoff, "The All-India Music Conferences of 1916–1925: Cultural Transformation and Colonial Ideology," *Hindustani Music*, ed. Bor et al., 331–356. On related developments in South India, see Indira Viswanathan Peterson and Davesh Soneji, eds., *Performing Pasts: Reinventing the Arts in Modern South India* (Oxford University Press, 2008); Davesh Soneji, *Unfinished Gestures:* Devadāsīs, *Memory, and Modernity in South India* (University of Chicago Press, 2012); Subramanian, *From the Tanjore Court*; Weidman, *Singing the Classical*.

11. Tejaswini Niranjana, *Musicophilia in Mumbai: Performing Subjects and the Metropolitan Unconscious* (Duke University Press, 2020); Pradhan, *Hindustani Music in Colonial Bombay*.
12. Satrangee Official, "Manali Bose sings 'Pal na laagi' in Raga Kalavati set to Teentaal (16 beats)," YouTube, May 8, 2021, educational video, https://www.youtube.com/watch?v=2EZJE4sNb4Q.
13. Morcom, *Illicit Worlds of Indian Dance*, 1–30.
14. Davesh Soneji, *Unbounded Tunes: Genealogies of Musical Pluralism in Modern South India* (forthcoming).
15. Partha Chatterjee, *The Nation and its Fragments: Colonial and Postcolonial Histories* (Princeton University Press, 1993), 73. For an excellent ethnomusicological discussion of Chatterjee's idea of the classicization of tradition, see Michael Largey, *Voudou Nation: Haitian Art Music and Cultural Nationalism* (University of Chicago Press, 2006), 18.
16. Metropolitan Museum of Art, "Tanpura Demonstration," YouTube, May 30, 2013, educational video, https://www.youtube.com/watch?v=rVeFX4O4zTo&list=PLB73DA5433C3A8C95&index=11.
17. वारकरी प्रवास, "How to Tune Tambora/Vina," YouTube, August 25, 2017, educational video, https://www.youtube.com/watch?v=C4FkMAPTS5M.
18. Amol Gavhane, "Pakhawaj playing - Rohan Dada Bhise (पखवाज वादन - रोहन दादा भिसे)," YouTube, November 2, 2023, educational video, https://www.youtube.com/watch?v=0NUe9YTN5eo.
19. Metropolitan Museum of Art, "Tabla: Theka, Qayeda, and Tukra in Tintal (Madhya Lay - Medium Tempo)," YouTube, May 30, 2013, educational video, https://www.youtube.com/watch?v=vlzeXCRh9QQ&list=PLB73DA5433C3A8C95&index=28.
20. Metropolitan Museum of Art, "Sarangi: Ektal Composition in Raag Desh, Ramesh Misra," YouTube, May 30, 2013, educational video, https://www.youtube.com/watch?v=Lc4i8TwZsHo&list=PLB73DA5433C3A8C95&index=52.

21. Dr. Sukhada Dandekar, "Keertan/Kirtan by Sukhada Dandekar (Vadodara) 25/12/2016," YouTube, November 13, 2017, educational video, https://www.youtube.com/watch?v=rlelASAdq2Y.
22. Classy Content, "#Kirtan Dattadasbuva ghag Part 01 (Purvaranga)," YouTube, June 12, 2021, educational video, 00:15–4:11, https://youtu.be/RExVNfNgoVk?si=HJ__MujsT7JygMUq. Please listen for H. Bh. P. Dattadasbuva Ghag, naman in Raga Kalavati (00:15–4:11) from his naradiya kirtan.
23. Jones, "Music, History, and the Sacred," 202.
24. *Dhrupad* is the oldest genre of vocal music within the Hindustani canon. Today, it is considered particularly austere.
25. Jacqueline Jones, "Performing the Sacred: Song, Genre, and Aesthetics in Bhakti" (PhD diss., University of Chicago, 2009); Anna Schultz, "The Livenesses of Pandit Bhimsen Joshi's Popular *Abhangas*," in *More than Bollywood: Studies in Indian Popular Music*, ed. Gregory D. Booth and Bradley Shope (Oxford University Press, 2014), 276–299; Jayson Beaster-Jones, *Music Commodities, Markets, and Values: Music as Merchandise* (Routledge, 2016), 111–140.
26. Bakhle, *Two Men and Music*, 140–143; Ashok Da. Ranade, "Keertana: An Effective Communication," in *On Music and Musicians of Hindoostan* (Promill, 1984), 109–140.
27. Bakhle, *Two Men and Music*, 8.
28. Ramkrishna Govindbuva Dhole, *Śrīharidāsa Govindatāraka Gīta va Pūrvāśramī Govindbuvā Hośiṅg Nāśikkar Yāñce Caritra* (Citrashāḷā Press, 1925).
29. Bakhle, *Two Men and Music*, 5, 124, 259; Katz, *Lineage of Loss*, 21; Subramaniam, *From the Tanjore Court*; Weidman, *Singing the Classical*, 5.
30. Ranade, "Keertana," 131.
31. Anna Schultz, *Singing a Hindu Nation: Marathi Devotional Performance and Nationalism* (Oxford University Press, 2013), 41–47; "Kirtan Sammelan," *Kesari*, Tuesday, January 15, 1918; *Kesari*, May 13, 1919, p. 7; "Fourth Kirtan Sammelan," *Kesari*, November 18, 1919, p. 7.
32. *Kesari*, February 8, 1921.
33. Govind Sakharam Sardesai, Introduction to Dhole, *Śrīharidāsa Govindatāraka*, 1.
34. Schultz, *Singing a Hindu Nation*, 30–32.
35. Adheesh A. Sathaye, *Crossing the Lines of Caste: Viśvāmitra and the Construction of Brahmin Power in Hindu Mythology* (Oxford University Press, 2015), 141.
36. A *linga* is an aniconic representation of Lord Shiva. The twelve important, ancient *Jyotirlinga* (*lingas* of light), are scattered throughout India and especially in the north. Angela Hohenberger, 'Liṅga,' in *Brill's Encyclopedia of Hinduism Online*, edited by Knut A. Jacobsen, Helene Basu, Angelika Malinar,

and Vasudha Narayanan (Brill, 2018), http://dx.doi.org/10.1163/2212-5019_BEH_COM_9000000175.

37. Dhole, *Śrīharidāsa Govindatāraka*, 1–3.
38. Dhole, *Śrīharidāsa Govindatāraka,* 1. This and most dates in the biography are listed according to the Hindu lunar calendar, in which Govindbuva's birth year is samvat 1870. The correspondence to the Gregorian calendar is imprecise, so it could be either 1813 or 1814.
39. A *gharana* (lit. "of the house") is a "family tradition; a stylistic school and/or the members of that school" (Daniel M. Neuman, *The Life of Music in North India: The Organization of an Artistic Tradition*, 2nd ed. [University of Chicago Press, 1990], 272). Gwalior is widely recognized as the oldest khayal *gharana*. It was founded by Haddu and Hassu Khan, court musicians for Shinde Maharaja of Gwalior. (Neuman, *Life of Music*, 148–49; Ranade, *Hindustani Music*, 93–94).
40. Dhole, *Śrīharidāsa Govindatāraka*, 9–12.
41. *Pakhawaj* is a double-headed barrel drum that was used to accompany both court and temple-based North Indian music in the nineteenth century.
42. "Remember the husband of Sita, praise Ram!" This *jayjaykar* (exclamation of praise) is performed at the beginning and ends of sections of a kirtan.
43. "*Tal*" in Marathi.
44. *Tambura* is a plucked string lute played as a drone instrument.
45. Marathi kirtan is a mixture of singing and speaking. The drums and cymbals are only played during song, while the string drone is heard throughout the kirtan, even when the kirtankar is speaking. What this story suggests is that Hoshing performed the entire akhyan of the kirtan in speech rather than song.
46. Dhole, *Śrīharidāsa Govindatāraka*, 10–12.
47. Dhole, *Śrīharidāsa Govindatāraka,* 20–38.
48. Sanskrit has a special connection with Brahminism; historically, only members of the Brahmin caste were permitted to learn Sanskrit and recite Sanskrit prayers during rituals. The latter practice continues until today.
49. "King," an honorific used to refer to kirtankars.
50. Worship rituals while reciting the Shrimad Bhagwat.
51. The *Shrimad Bhagavata* (also called *Bhagavata Purana*) is an ancient Sanskrit religious text.
52. To receive darshan is to see and be seen by the divine.
53. Manakirnaka *snan*: A ritual bath in the Manakarnika, a sacred pool of the Ganges river in Varanasi.

54. *Madhyanha sandhya*.
55. *Brahmayadnya*: Worshipping God through offerings of water.
56. *Sāyamsandhyā*.
57. Pandharpur is a major pilgrimage center in southern Maharashtra and home to the main temple of Lord Vitthala.
58. Dhole, *Śrīharidāsa Govindatāraka,* 23. *Chaturmas* is a period of four holy months in the lunar calendar in which devout Hindus fast, bathe in holy rivers, and observe austerities and rituals.
59. Dhole, *Śrīharidāsa Govindatāraka*, 24–30; Viyaja R. Scindia, *The Last Maharani of Gwalior: An Autobiography* (SUNY Press, 1987), 91.
60. Barbara N. Ramusack, *The Indian Princes and their States* (Cambridge University Press, 2003), 35.
61. Justin Scarimbolo, "Brahmans Beyond Nationalism, Muslims Beyond Dominance: A Hidden History of North Indian Classical Music's Hinduization" (PhD diss., University of California, Santa Barbara, 2014).
62. "*Wa!*" is an exclamation of appreciation uttered by listeners to classical music (used like "Bravo!").
63. *Khudā*: A Persian word for the Almighty.
64. "Salaam" is the Islamicate term for a deep bow. When speaking of Hindus, the term "*namaskar*" is more typical.
65. Mayuresh Kadu, "KeertanRang (Part 1) by Charudatta Aphale," SoundCloud, June 15, 2014, sound recording, 11:07–14:25 ("Balkrishna Charani"), https://on.soundcloud.com/ByrfYsFk7m4iouAH6.
66. Dhole, *Śrīharidāsa Govindatāraka,* 27.
67. Dhole, *Śrīharidāsa Govindatāraka,* 27–30.
68. Bakhle, *Two Men and Music*, 141; Wim van der Meer, *Hindustani Music in the 20th Century* (Martinus Nijhoff, 1980), 132; Neuman, *Life of Music*, 105.
69. Kadu, "KeertanRang (Part I) Charudatta Aphale," https://on.soundcloud.com/ByrfYsFk7m4iouAH6, 11:07–14:25.
70. Classy Content, "H. B. P. Ramchandrabuva karhadkar – Sitaram charani laksha lago," YouTube, April 4, 2020, educational video, https://www.youtube.com/watch?v=5qTY7SEgCCg.
71. Scarimbolo, "Brahmans Beyond Nationalism."
72. Dhole, *Śrīharidāsa Govindatāraka*, 7–9, 20–21, 36–37.
73. Dhole, *Śrīharidāsa Govindatāraka*, 7–9, 30–37.
74. Ranade, "Keertana," 130–132.
75. Ranade, "Keertana," 13; Dhole, *Śrīharidāsa Govindatāraka*, 38–39, 46–56; Schultz, *Singing a Hindu Nation*, 30–32.

76. Schultz, *Singing a Hindu Nation,* 33–34.
77. Although naradiya kirtankars absorb the sounds of Hindustani music while rejecting the label “classical,” Hindustani musicians have by and large not appropriated the genres—the *naman, arya, saki, dindi*, etc.—of naradiya kirtan. Naradiya kirtan, already populated by Brahmins, authorized by Brahminical scriptural knowledge, and ripe with sonic classicism, left little for Brahmin nationalists and classicizers to reform. Schultz, *Singing a Hindu Nation*, 13–14.
78. “Communalism” is a term used within South Asia to refer to inter-religious or inter-ethnic strife, especially between Hindus and Muslims.

CHAPTER FOUR

THINKING ABOUT MUSIC HISTORY

An Introduction to Marxism

Marianna Ritchey

I've always felt a bit like an outsider in musicology. Initially this was because, unlike many people in my field, I didn't grow up playing or knowing anything about classical music. My most formative early musical encounter was discovering They Might Be Giants in seventh grade, and although I grew up taking piano lessons, my performance experience has mostly been as a drummer and singer in various punk-adjacent bands. Then in my late twenties I decided to get a PhD in musicology, because I had had a fantastic music history professor in college, and it gave me the idea that I might be suited for such a career. In grad school, despite not having a classical background, I specialized in nineteenth-century European art music, a decision I still can't totally explain. As a relative latecomer to this world, I find lots of things about it confusing, and this confusion has ended up generating most of my scholarship since grad school.

One of the things that has confused me is the general lack of a widespread musicological consideration of capitalism, when it comes to understanding this music and its history (and its present). Until recently, the most serious studies of capitalism and music were undertaken by Theodor W. Adorno and Hans Eisler, who weren't musicologists (they were a sociologist and a film theorist, respectively).[1] *In the 1990s, musicologists drew on Adorno's work in order to bring analyses of gender, sexuality, and race into the field, but capitalism as a topic of serious study remains only sporadically addressed even today (although this has been changing in recent years, and I have put some examples of this change in my list of reading suggestions at the end of this essay). Given that so many people outside musicology consider gender and race to be entangled with class and thus with capitalism, this blind spot in the field seems odd. There are probably several reasons for it, but one reason I've been interested in has to do with the fundamentally idealist worldview of this specific corner of the musical world. And this gets me to what this essay is really about, which is introducing you to Marxism.*

Marxism isn't exactly a political orientation, the way communism or anarchism or fascism are, although it does require a critical attitude toward capitalism. Marxism is more correctly understood as an analytical *method*, meaning a way of investigating and interpreting something. The work of Karl Marx has a reputation for being difficult to read, and some sections of his writings certainly are. But I think that some of the general outlines of what he did and why it matters aren't actually that complicated to deal with. In this essay I'm going to talk a bit about why I think Marx is interesting and useful, some of his key insights, and some ways later Marxists have expanded on his theories. I'll include a short example from my own work, where I use an essentially Marxist framework to try to understand the problem of racism and/in US classical music with a different kind of critical nuance than other frameworks allow. The Marxist way of thinking can be applied to many things you may want to understand, including music, and my goal here is to give you a way in to this mode of analysis.

To put it succinctly, Marx just wanted to really understand capitalism from top to bottom. Most people, including many economists, then and now, don't actually understand capitalism, and aren't even that interested in it—not really. They tend to think of it as a system of rules and functions to master (supply and demand, laws of competition, interest rates, monetary policy, and so on) that are more or less detached from actual lived reality. They often describe the economy as though it has nothing to do with culture, or people's actions, or anything other than politically neutral laws of math. But this impression—that economists are politically and morally neutral—is false. For example, when economists and finance analysts state that capitalism has raised the standard of living for everyone on earth, or when they point out that preventing mass deaths in a pandemic would be bad for the economy, or that devastating wars are good for it, they aren't being neutral at all.[2] Instead, they're actually revealing a lot about their moral perspective, and working hard to uphold very specific political situations.

A Marxist orientation toward economic questions differs from mainstream economics in this way. Marx wanted to understand capitalism in its entirety, as a whole interlocking social, political, and economic system that shapes, and is shaped by, people's beliefs and relationships and feelings and moral codes, and how we experience work and family and consumption, and how we relate to the earth. While later Marxist and post-Marxist theorists have extended and debated many of his theories, his basic explanation remains a useful starting place for developing a critique of capitalism to this day. In US business or economics classes, you are unlikely to learn much about Marx, because the job of those fields is to make capitalism seem benign and rational, whereas Marx demonstrates the opposite. I think it's the responsibility of everyone who lives in this system to clearly see it for what it is. For one thing, anyone who cares about social justice needs to develop a deep understanding of how social problems are produced or intensified by capitalism, as I will address below.

Capitalism is a relatively recent development in human history, emerging roughly in the sixteenth century in Western Europe (so, for starters, it's interesting to me, as a musicologist, to note that the beginnings of what we broadly consider to be "classical music" map so closely onto the time and place of capitalism's emergence).[3] Marx set out to understand why and how this emergence happened. What historical conditions had to be in place for this epochal transformation in world economic relations to occur? And, crucially, what historical conditions will have to be in place for capitalism to one day be overcome?

His lifetime of work developing answers to these questions spanned roughly the 1840s to 1880s and includes several books, many lengthy essays, and the three volumes of *Capital* itself (Volume 1 was published in 1867; the other two volumes were compiled from his notes and published after his death by his soulmate Friedrich Engels). In *Capital* Marx pursues a sustained argument with the previous generation of political economists who had first tried to explain capitalism in the eighteenth century, people like Adam Smith and David Ricardo and other Enlightenment thinkers you may know. This loosely aligned group observed the fall of age-old hierarchies of inherited wealth and privilege, which were somehow being destroyed by this emerging thing called a "market economy." How, they wondered, were all these random lower-class merchants and Swiss banks somehow amassing more economic power than the King of Spain? How did it happen?

Many economic thinkers of the eighteenth century were interested in ways the emerging form of capitalism could potentially make individuals freer to act on their own terms, economically. Eventually, the kinds of economists who emphasized the associations between the capitalist system and individual freedom started being called liberals. Today, liberals are still people who center their understanding of a free society on individual rights and personal freedoms, and who believe Western capitalist democracy is the best system for ensuring those rights and freedoms. In short, liberal political theory and the capitalist economy developed together and continue to reinforce each other. One of the things that Marx seeks to uncover is the way seemingly unobjectionable liberal beliefs in things like freedom and equality are nonetheless shaped in ways that support capitalism, with all its unfreedoms and inequalities.

Marx did this by reading the eighteenth-century economists *critically*; that is, with an eye toward contradictions and unaddressed failures of logic, in order to reveal how much *ideology* is at work in their explanations. In this sense, ideology means you are arranging facts in order to support some deeply held belief you may not even be fully aware you hold. For just one example: liberal economists tend to take for granted the notion that humans are "by nature" competitive and self-serving. This probably just sounds like a commonsense fact you have heard your whole life, but it's really an *ideological statement*. There's no empirical proof that it's true, and in fact if you actually look at the full span of human history it's a lot easier to prove the *opposite* claim: that while humans, like many animals, are of course sometimes violent, we are also cooperative and mutually supporting in an incredible variety of ways, and indeed this is why and how societies exist in the first place.[4] But it's no accident that the former belief, about our natural brutal competitiveness, is the one that circulates so widely in US culture. It's because that belief justifies capitalism, a dog-eat-dog system based on ruthless individual competition, with police and jails to keep our supposed selfish natural instincts in check. How convenient, that this system, which is only a few hundred years old, turns out to be the ideal one for managing the essential biological "nature" of our entire species! Marx looks at claims like these and rolls his eyes.

As you may have picked up on by now, one of the reasons *Capital* is so long and complicated is because Marx believed capitalism can't be understood without understanding everything else in the world. I'm not joking—he famously described his method as "the ruthless criticism of everything in existence."[5] For this reason, his work doesn't fit neatly into any disciplinary category. He interweaves pages and pages of extremely boring mathematical equations with close readings of eighteenth-century political theory, excerpts from medical treatises, and quotations from Goethe and Shakespeare. When describing the parasitic nature of capital, Marx suddenly starts talking about vampires and werewolves. Sometimes he's very funny, like when he pretends to espouse the fatuous arguments of economists and parliamentarians he despises. In short, *Capital* is a very weird product, but it's also an incredibly rich and provocative one.

Here are a few Marxist terms and concepts that I think can help us get a general idea of what his method is like, and why it might be useful to apply it to music history.

Means of Production

What are the "means" by which we "produce" all the stuff we produce? The means of production are things like factories, farms, laboratories, and mines (and also *land,* which I will address below). Marx is specifically interested in who *owns* the means of production in a given type of society. In some societies they may be "collectively" owned, meaning everyone owns them; in others they may be "nationalized," meaning the government owns them. Under capitalism, the means of production are privately owned, by individual capitalists and corporations.

Private Property

I just used the phrase "privately owned," which gets us into the often misunderstood concept of "private property." Private property is *not* things like your toothbrush or TV (those things are just personal property). Private property refers specifically to property that generates profit somehow. A factory is private property. Land you rent out is private property. One of the many ways that Marx's description of capitalism is more precise and interesting than those of conventional economists is that he understood private property as a *social relation*, not just as a static thing. There's nothing about a factory or a segment of land that inherently designates it to be private property. That designation emerges out of the social relations of the people who interact with the factory or the land. These are the "property relations" Marx writes about. If I own a factory and pay you to work at it, the profits from what you produce go to me, even though it was your labor that generated them. A house I rent out to you is also private property; in that case I'm profiting off the labor you did to earn the money you then pay to me in rent. Both cases describe a social relationship between you and me that requires an entire apparatus of laws, beliefs, and rights to uphold. Capitalism depends on these relations of private property, and these relations shape our worldviews and value systems in all kinds of significant ways. This is why communists talk about abolishing private property, and it's why capitalists fixate on protecting private property.

The history of private property is tangled up with the changing role of land. In feudal England, there was not yet an established system of private property in the capitalist sense. Land was seen as territory, and as the place where food and other subsistence comes from, but it was not yet a generator of financial profit, and the lord was not really considered its owner, in the modern senses of those terms.

Instead, much of feudal Europe (at least, the aspect of feudal Europe Marx was interested in) was characterized by a particular type of land relation that is almost nonexistent in the United States today: *the commons*. In the old feudal manorial system, rural land was generally apportioned in three main ways: there was land owned by a lord (hence today's term, landlord); there were plots of land that belonged to the peasants who lived in villages within a particular lord's jurisdiction; and there were "the commons," which were lands held in common by the people of that village. These common lands emerged out of very complex histories of class struggle between peasants, lords, petty artisans, and the church. There were lots of complicated (and shifting) laws regarding them, and these laws functioned differently in different times and places. But for our purposes I will emphasize the feature of the commons that has been most interesting to Marxist scholars: namely, the role the commons played in the class struggle between peasants and lords. In many contexts, the commons served as a sort of safety net, where people were able to hunt, fish, chop down wood, and even live, if need be. Some scholars, like Silvia Federici, have argued that the commons thus acted as a kind of bulwark protecting peasants from total exploitation and abuse by their lords, because the existence of the commons made it more difficult for the ruling classes to use the threat of starvation to force the peasantry to do things. In this respect, peasants often weren't wholly dependent on their lord, and their lord could only push them so far.

The commons were thus a hotly contested arena for class struggle during the transition to capitalism. Because of lots of incredibly complicated changes in the wool industry (and other issues that Marx describes in great detail in *Capital*, Volume 1), beginning in the sixteenth century, the rising class of proto-capitalists colluded to violently evict all the peasants off most of the land in the British Isles, and increasingly across western Europe (and the whole rest of the world, via colonialism). They kicked them out of their villages and, furthermore, enclosed the commons and turned them into private property: property it was now illegal to hunt or fish or collect wood on. The enclosure of the commons generated widespread famine and forced migration, and led to the imposition of new, incredibly brutal laws criminalizing vagrancy. Vast numbers of displaced starving peasants thus had no choice but to move to cities and become workers in the new factories that were rising up to replace the old networks of artisanal guild labor that had previously characterized urban production. Marx called this historical process the "proletarianization" of the feudal agricultural peasantry into something totally new, called *the working class*.

Labor

What defines the working class is the type of labor it does, which is *wage labor*. In the United States, we often seem to talk about class as though it has to do with relative wealth: if you or your family have a lot of money, you are considered upper class, and if you don't have much money, you're working class. But that isn't actually the definition of class that's been outlined by Marxists. In the Marxist sense, the working class is all of the people who do not own the means of production (factories, record labels, orchestras, restaurants, universities), and who must thus secure wage labor from a capitalist or from a business in order to survive. In that sense, even people with a lot of relative wealth and privilege are still technically working class, insofar as they are beholden to a boss for a paycheck. This is the great political value inherent in Marxist class theory: it provides a potential for a kind of mass collective identification, and the awareness that we all have certain shared political concerns, despite the many other differences and conflicts that exist between different groups of us.

This form of labor—this labor *relation,* the "wage relation"—is part of what makes capitalism possible. Capitalism organized productive work differently than it had ever been organized before, whether during feudalism or any other previous form of society anywhere else in the world (and there have been a countless variety of social organizational forms over the past three hundred thousand years that *Homo sapiens* has existed).[6] Under European feudalism, for example, money existed but was rarely a primary form of exchange. Peasants worked a lord's land in exchange for being allowed to live on it and also grow their *own* crops and graze their *own* cows on it. Meaning, their rent and taxes were paid mainly in the form of direct labor and of a percentage of the products they grew and made for themselves. Under capitalism, however, this all goes away and everyone has to get paid, and pay for stuff, solely in the form of money. This makes all kinds of new things possible, but it also causes all kinds of new problems.

For one thing, wage labor required people to radically change the way they experienced time. Outside the conditions imposed on us by capitalism, people do work when the work needs to be done: the cows need milking when their udders are full; the grain needs to be harvested when it's ripe; a pair of new socks needs to get knitted when the old pair wears out. In other words, work is thought of primarily in terms of the product being created when it makes sense to create it, and its relative direct usefulness to whoever needs it. Under conditions like these, work varies widely from season to season and place to place. Under such conditions, if you were going to use money to buy someone's labor, you'd either buy a whole person (a slave) who would then do all this productive work for you, or you'd use money (or barter something) to acquire a product a person had made with their own labor. Both these ways of paying for the labor of others have existed, in various forms and places, probably more or less forever. But wage labor—that is, *renting* a person's body for a set number of hours, having them do various, even radically unrelated things (or even nothing) during those hours, and then breaking up their payment into a certain equal amount of money per hour—is extremely bizarre historically. It forces workers to relate to the passage of time, and to our own labor processes, and even to our own bodies, in a very abstracted and unnatural way.

Marx wanted to understand why this transformation was so necessary. Why does capitalism require wage labor and adherence to clock time? Boiled down, his argument is basically that hourly wage labor is what makes profit possible, in the capitalist sense of the term, where somehow a capitalist pays you to work for them and then they end up with more money than they paid you for your work.

I am skipping and simplifying huge chunks of Marx's argument (and I'm not even touching on his ideas about *commodity fetishism*, which comprise some of the most interesting sections of *Capital*),[7] but for brevity's sake we can just remember this: capitalism happens (a) when everything is turned into private property, such that the means of production are owned by just a few individuals and no one else has access to them; and (b) when productive labor is organized via time-based wages.

Freedom

His discussion of the enclosure of the commons and of wage labor leads Marx to some big conclusions about how freedom is conceived within liberal political theory. Wage labor is one of the main reasons liberals say individuals are more free under capitalism than they are under other economic models like communism or slavery. In pre- or non-capitalist cultures, people directly produce their own subsistence, whether as hunter-gatherers, tenant farmers, nomadic herders, or any number of other lifeways. But in capitalist countries like the United States, you're essentially not allowed to live, hunt, grow food, or graze animals *anywhere* unless you own (or rent) that land, because almost *everything* has been enclosed and made into private property. There are even parts of the United States where collecting rainwater in your own yard is restricted, because that water "belongs" to the ranchers who have purchased "water rights" from the state.[8] Imagine what a feudal peasant would have thought about that! At any rate, now, instead of having direct access to all the stuff we would normally use to produce our own survival, most of us have to rent our bodies out to capitalists for set numbers of hours in order to receive *wages*, which we then give to *other* capitalists in order to *buy* (or rent, as with housing) our means of survival from them, thus further enriching those capitalists as well. When you put it this way, it sounds pretty bad. But because we aren't literally forced to work—because this isn't slavery, where somebody with a whip directly makes you do things—liberal theorists see waged labor as "free labor," meaning, labor we do by choice.

This is kind of a complicated argument, but it's important, so I will restate it: To put it bluntly, Marx shows that the liberal conception of "individual freedom" relies on *depriving people of their ability to directly support themselves and each other.* Now that we are no longer allowed to produce our own subsistence, and have been made wholly dependent on convincing a capitalist to pay us wages if we want to survive, we are told that we have been made free. Marx wants us to notice these contradictions and to realize that the way liberals talk about freedom is thus *ideological.* It serves ruling-class interests, which is to say capitalist-class interests.

Finally, here are two big words that are useful for understanding Marxism and my little sketch of a Marxist critique of classical music that follows.

Idealism is a perspective that many of the people reading this are probably comfortable with, whether you are conscious of it or not, because it's the one that has shaped a lot of what we call Western culture for many centuries. Idealism is the belief that most things of importance happen in the mind; for example, historical change happens because people's ideas change. Liberals tend to be idealists who see liberalism primarily as a new set of ideas (about human rights, freedom, individual liberty, and democracy) that swept across Europe and increasingly around the world. They usually believe that these new ideas then generated new economic, social, political, and juridical relations. This is probably a story you know well.

Materialism is the frame that Marx constructs to combat this idealist perspective. Of course, ideas are real, and they do participate in shaping reality, as he was perfectly aware; it's just that for him they aren't *primary.*

For starters, he notes that in order to have ideas in the first place, you have to be alive, which means you have to have food and clothes and a place to sleep, you have to have been raised by somebody, and so on. Meaning, the things you're able to think about are always inextricable from your material conditions. To use his word—an important word for Marxists—we would say that ideas and material conditions have a *dialectical* relationship.[9] Dialectical, in the Marxist sense, means that ideas and material reality are mutually constitutive. Ideas don't come first and then generate material change, or vice versa. Rather, ideas and material conditions evolve together, constantly influencing and being influenced by each other. For example, not only could a Neolithic human not have *built* a car, they couldn't have even had the *idea* of a car. The material conditions that could lead to the idea of the car (metalwork, machine production, gasoline, internal combustion, a particular society in which traveling far and fast is a good thing to do, and the rest) were nonexistent for them. And similarly, a Neolithic person certainly had all kinds of ideas that you and I can no longer have, because our conditions are so radically different. Mapping this onto music, we can consider the fact that a Neolithic person could not have written a piano sonata, not because they weren't smart or advanced or civilized enough—as perhaps conventional ways of understanding history might have taught us—but because they occupied totally different material conditions than those that produced the piano sonata. To have piano sonatas, you have to have pianos (which would require metalwork, woodwork, nuts and bolts, a non-nomadic society in which "houses" means buildings with floors strong enough to support massive weight) as well as paper, ink, musical notation, fixed tuning systems, and a desire for polyphony, not to mention an understanding of music as something encoded onto paper by an individual mind (which is not a very historically common way of understanding music). Meanwhile, Neolithic people didn't have any of these particular things, values, or desires, but *did* have vast networks of *other* things, values, and desires, which surely led to sonic practices we can't imagine or even begin to recreate. In short, our ideas and perspectives are the way they are because of the material conditions we live in, but at the same time those conditions are obviously influenced by things we think about and then bring into reality.

Whether you have a materialist or an idealist worldview will drastically shape how you envision political change and activism. For an idealist, ending problems like racism or climate change become formulated mainly in terms of getting more people to think better thoughts. A materialist, by contrast, will try to understand the larger context of such problems, the way that context *shapes* the thoughts people think about the problems, and the ways this is all tangled up with money and power and institutional profits. So, for a Marxist, ideas and feelings are important, but focusing too exclusively on them obscures a full comprehension of material reality that is crucial for developing appropriate actions toward political change. People's feelings don't change the world, their *actions* do, and the line supposedly connecting feelings to actions is not always very strong or clear.

MUSICAL IDEALISM AND RACISM: A QUICK CASE STUDY

What could it look like, to examine music and music history through a Marxist lens? Here is one quick example of something I've been working on in my research, and which draws on some of the concepts outlined above.

I would say that Western European classical music—and the musicology that studies it—tends to be idealist in its orientation toward knowledge. Open up a "History of Western Music" textbook (or most music appreciation textbooks), and you will probably see a chronological story of individuals who use their creative insights to overcome problems, often through reasoned debate with other individuals. You will see a focus on individual composers and their creative ideas, rather than on the performers whose labor realizes those ideas, to say nothing of the people who make violins or the construction workers who build opera houses. Somehow those things don't really feel like music history. Learning about music history in this culture usually means studying scores and the content of compositions. In other words, our object of study isn't people, it's the ideas and content created by people, which isn't quite the same thing.

The way the problems of racism and sexism are named, in US classical music culture, similarly centers content and individuals: the canon of great composers is all white men, the vast majority of works programmed at our elite performance venues are by white men, and even orchestras and audiences are predominantly white. As classical music institutions increasingly come under fire for these glaringly uneven statistics, their leaders—as well as regular artists involved in this culture, and musicologists too—are trying to figure out what ought to be done.

After the racial justice uprisings of 2020, many of these institutions undertook significant diversity and public outreach initiatives aimed at addressing racism. For example, in its 2021 diversity statement Lincoln Center (home of the Metropolitan Opera and the New York Philharmonic, as well as the Juilliard School) proclaimed its new goal to ensure "that everyone—regardless of identity, ability, background, or personal experience—belongs at Lincoln Center."[10] They pledged to do things like implement music education programs in underserved public schools, program more works by non-white composers, and hire more non-white people into positions of power in the institution. All of these moves are generally seen as a healthy way of reckoning with the racist past of the institution and of classical music generally.

But a Marxist would read this discourse critically, putting it up against the material history (and present) of classical institutions to see where contradictions or evasions manifest, in an effort to understand the full extent of the problem that these diversity initiatives think they are solving. For example, we might consider the possibility that institutional racism doesn't have to do solely with the artistic content such institutions showcase or because of the lack of individual identity-based diversity on their governing boards. Additionally, analyzing networks of money and power can reveal a more materially significant role these institutions play in white supremacy. This role has to do with things like the investment activities of their billionaire funders, and the way they serve as tax shelters and reputation-laundering mechanisms for covering up the more unsavory activities of some of those funders.[11] It also has to do with the literal construction and location of these buildings.

Lincoln Center was completed in 1965. Its creation served as what urban planning scholar David Wilson calls "the redevelopment cornerstone" of the project to clean up Manhattan's slums and bring "private-sector reinvestment" to the Upper West Side neighborhood during the postwar period.[12] During this time the federal government created sweeping new legislation and earmarked huge amounts of funds intended to allow cities to build new highways and modernize public housing. What this looked like in practice was that city governments all across the United States used the new law of eminent domain to kick thousands of poor people—disproportionately but not exclusively people of color—out of their homes, bulldozing their neighborhoods into rubble, thus freeing these areas up for lucrative new real estate developments.

"High culture" institutions like concert halls and art museums have often played major roles in these redevelopment projects because of their ability to raise the class profile of an area and draw in tourists under the seemingly socially beneficial banner of bringing art and culture to an underserved neighborhood.[13] In the earlier part of the twentieth century, the Upper West Side of Manhattan held many of the city's Black inhabitants and was home to a thriving Black business district as well as many jazz clubs. But this isn't the kind of art and culture that attracts top-dollar real estate investments. So, after the city evicted around seven thousand Black families from their homes, and then razed those homes, as well as hundreds of businesses and music clubs, to the ground, Lincoln Center was built in their place, and was then celebrated for revitalizing the area by bringing art to it. Today, "Jazz at Lincoln Center" is even celebrated for "preserving America's jazz heritage" on the very location where living jazz once reverberated out of Black-owned music venues and nightclubs.[14]

Now, the people at Lincoln Center tell us that the racial inequality this institution played such a *material* role in creating can be addressed by the institution itself. But will this restitution come in a similarly material form? For example, will representatives of Lincoln Center track down the seven thousand families the institution displaced, and give them all of the wealth in Lincoln Center's stock portfolios? No, it means they will make Lincoln Center itself more "accessible" to people who have historically been excluded from consuming and making the high culture it circulates and safeguards. This will be accomplished by identifying certain exceptional (usually also meaning exceptionally wealth-privileged) members of marginalized identity groups and—in the words of Lincoln Center's diversity statement—lift "the best and brightest" of them "into our world." In other words, classical music will solve racism by helping more people participate in it, which is an approach to racial justice that also conveniently serves Lincoln Center itself, by broadening its potential consumer base.

Black radical thinkers and revolutionaries like W. E. B. Du Bois, Cedric Robinson, Angela Davis, and many others have extended and nuanced Marx's fundamental insights in order to convincingly argue that racism is, has always been, and will always be an inextricable aspect of capitalism (this is what the term "racial capitalism," made famous by Robinson, is intended to gloss).[15] The capitalist system, we should remember, only exists thanks to a situation where a few people own all the means of production, and the majority of people must do wage labor in order to survive. This means that capitalism *requires* inequality. These thinkers argue that the creation of racist hierarchies (indeed, the creation of racial categories themselves) has thus always been a necessary aspect of capitalism, because the system needs a large, desperate, propertyless underclass (a population that people in more privileged positions also see as inferior, less capable, less human) in order to keep labor costs low. As Jodi Melamed puts it, "racism enshrines the inequality that capitalism requires."[16] If this is true, then it throws idealist attempts to end racism by changing what music people listen to, or who gets to play it, into a new light. Such changes may be helpful to some marginalized individuals, and they may create concert programming that's more interesting to listen to. There may be good enough reasons, on their own, to pursue these changes. But what a materialist analysis shows us is that these changes in themselves will never end racism in its true form as an aspect of the system we live in, and if that's their stated goal then something else must be going on. Indeed, you could argue that such activities make the general situation worse, by giving the *impression* that they are ending racism, even as the fundamental system of racialized domination and exploitation/extraction that makes our society function—and thanks to which these institutions continue to reap profits—remains completely intact.

One reason a lot of people don't like this kind of argument is that it doesn't offer easy ways out. What are the people inside of Lincoln Center supposed to do? The philosopher Olúfẹ́mi O. Táíwò argues that elite institutions like classical concert halls (or universities, the main subject of his book) really *can't* do anything other than make idealist moves toward diversifying programming and governing boards.[17] Their existence is contingent on a hierarchical society in which some people are rich and most people are poor. Given this fact, there's only so much that well-meaning people inside of these institutions can do. Táíwò thinks that honestly acknowledging this can help us come up with better ideas for addressing social problems than the standard ones our institutions promote. It might help us look for interesting political work to do outside of these institutions, for example. In other words, understanding that social liberation will not come from the top down is a clearer way of seeing things, and this clearer way will lead us to better decisions when we strive for liberation. Elite institutions are only able to package such liberation in forms that will continue to serve those institutions. That's always their main goal, because it has to be; that's what an institution is, at least under capitalism.

Táíwò's book is a beautiful example of how Marxist arguments and perspectives have proliferated and multiplied in the one hundred and forty years since Marx's death. Marxism is like a toolbox full of tools, and tools can always be sharpened and improved upon. For example, I've developed my analyses of classical music and gentrification by reading Marx's history of private property, where the wealthy class kicked all the poor people off all the land and scooped it up for their own use. But later and ongoing work by Black and Indigenous thinkers who extended or complicated or even disagreed with his theories has been equally—probably even more—important to me as I've struggled to develop my own perspective. Where Marx believed that land dispossession constituted an important first step in the consolidation of capitalism, one that eventually comes to an end, these future thinkers instead prove that land dispossession is a constant feature of capitalism in *all* its historical phases. In short, by centering race and colonialism in their analyses to an extent that Marx didn't, such thinkers have been able to see things differently than he did, which then enables them to construct a differently nuanced portrait of capitalism, while still taking his fundamental observations about class and exploitation and land dispossession as starting points. Thanks to these extensions of Marx, it becomes easier to see the construction of Lincoln Center as just one part of a centuries-long, and still ongoing, historical process, one that programming different kinds of symphonies will never stop.

CONCLUSIONS

I've touched on only a few of the ideas you encounter when you read Marx, and only a few of the ways you can use, elaborate on, and extend those ideas to understand the things you want to understand about the world. There are many other directions that a Marxist investigation of music or music history could take. What kind of labor (in the Marxist sense) is composing versus performing versus violin-making? How did the template for modern concert halls develop, and in what ways has that template shaped musical practice? What else is there to say about racism and/in music, from a materialist perspective? Or sexism, or ableism? How would a Marxist think about the institutional world of awards and commissions that so much classical music in the United States depends on? How would a Marxist understand the US tax code, which makes donations to orchestras and opera companies tax deductible? In what ways do these musical institutions and their funding models serve power? You could even take your Marxist toolbox into more eccentric arenas. For example, you could notice Marx's suggestion in the *Grundrisse* that artistic creation represents free labor in a capitalist system where so much labor is unfree.[18] I tried to explore this suggestion in an article I wrote a few years ago, but there are other ways you could fit music into Marx's picture of free labor.[19] These kinds of questions are not just for classical music, either—I mostly think about classical music in my research, and that's how I oriented this essay. But you could use material analysis to ask questions about any music you want. For example, how do digital and online technologies shape musical practices? Who developed those technologies and why, and who profits off them, if it's not artists? Or, what might be gained from examining huge global pop stars like Taylor Swift or Beyoncé via a Marxist understanding of how the commodity form contributes to alienation? Does music have use-value, in the Marxist sense, and if so, what might that consist of? Finally, it would be interesting to try to analyze music itself—any music—through some sort of Marxist lens. Adorno did this in the earlier twentieth century, with Western classical music, and more recent scholars have also made attempts along these lines, but are there different ways we could take on such a task, and would the task look different depending on which music we chose to analyze?[20] I've given some examples of Marxist musicological work in the brief bibliography below. Reading them will give you more ideas for how you could apply Marxist analysis and perspectives to the music topics you're interested in.

My hope is that you'll decide Marx is interesting and start reading him, but I think it's just as great if you instead go read the work of some other Marxist who you feel speaks more directly to what you're interested in. I myself first came to Marx through reading Silvia Federici's book *Caliban and the Witch,* which retells the story of capitalism by centering gender roles, misogyny, and the unpaid labor of women rather than the exploited labor of factory workers. Marx was interested in what happens when labor becomes waged, but Federici is interested in all the labor that *never did* become waged, and how it too is crucial for the emergence and continuation of capitalism.

Just as with post-Marxist theories about racism, Federici's decision to center women and domestic work allows her to tell the story of the transition from feudalism to capitalism in a very different way than the way Marx tells it, while her method is still recognizably Marxist. Struggling to read this book, and slowly becoming more and more upset as I came to understand what Federici was saying, really changed my life. The more stuff like this you read, the clearer things become, and the easier it is to keep reading even more of it. I think of this process as a journey of discovery, one that links you up with people all around the world, people dead and people living, all of whom, like you, just want the world to be a better place for everyone to live in, and want to think together—honestly, clearly, and not without difficulty and struggle—about how we might accomplish that goal.

Following is a very short selected list of some things you might enjoy if you thought anything in this essay was interesting.

NOTES

1. Timothy Taylor describes this lacuna in musicology at greater length in the first chapter of his book *Music and Capitalism: A History of the Present* (University of Chicago Press, 2015).
2. Rainer Zitelmann, "Anyone Who Doesn't Know the Following Facts About Capitalism Should Learn Them," Forbes, (July 27, 2020), https://www.forbes.com/sites/rainerzitelmann/2020/07/27/anyone-who-doesnt-know-the-following-facts-about-capitalism-should-learn-them/?sh=57704b433dc1; Ann Saphir and Jeff Mason, "The U.S. Weighs the Grim Math of Death vs. the Economy," Reuters, March 30, 2020, https://www.reuters.com/article/us-health-coronavirus-usa-reopen-analysi/the-u-s-weighs-the-grim-math-of-death-vs-the-economy-idUSKBN21H1B4/; Peter Pham, "Is War Good for Economies?" Forbes, November 6, 2017, https://www.forbes.com/sites/peterpham/2017/11/06/is-war-good-for-economies/?sh=56e5b8db4d9d.
3. For a canonical explanation of the history of capitalism see Ellen Meiksins Wood, *The Origin of Capitalism: A Longer View* (Verso, 2002). For a very short and readable essay exploring some of the ways capitalism works on, in, and with historical developments we might not think of as particularly related to capitalism, see Derek Ford, "The Base-Superstructure: A Model for Analysis and Action," *Liberation School* (November 22, 2021), https://www.liberationschool.org/base-superstructure-introduction/, accessed July 3, 2024.
4. In fact, many scientists and philosophers in the nineteenth century came to drastically different conclusions than Darwin did about the role competition plays in evolution. Darwin's most famous critic along these lines was

the Russian anarchist Peter Kropotkin, who coined the term "mutual aid" to describe the fundamentally important role that cooperation and coordination have played in human development and evolution. See, in particular, his book *The Conquest of Bread* (1892) and his collection of essays *Mutual Aid: A Factor of Evolution* (published individually 1890–96, collected in 1902).

5. Karl Marx, Letter to Arnold Ruge, September 1843, *Deutsch-Französische Jahrbücher*, February 1844.
6. Marx's work is highly Eurocentric. As the Black radical theorist Walter Rodney puts it, Marx was studying his own time, place, and culture, and the value of his work to revolutionary decolonial movements around the world is twofold: on the one hand, Marx's work provides invaluable insight into the European culture that enslaved and colonized the rest of the world, and such insight is helpful for revolutionary struggles against this culture; and on the other hand, although people in different countries are shaped by different cultures and conditions and have different histories, "we are all in one way or another located within the capitalist system of production," which Marx's analytical method helps us clearly see and comprehend. For Rodney's arguments about how and why Marx is useful to decolonial struggle despite primarily writing about Europe, see Walter Rodney, *Decolonial Marxism: Essays from the Pan-African Revolution*, eds. Asha Rodney, Patricia Rodney, Ben Mabie, and Jesse Benjamin (Verso, 2022).
7. Karl Marx, *Capital, Volume 1*, Chapter One, Section Four: "The Fetishism of Commodities and the Secret Thereof" (1867, edition in English 1887), translated by Samuel Moore and Edward Aveling, edited by Friedrich Engels, https://www.marxists.org/archive/marx/works/1867-c1/ch01.htm#S4, accessed July 3, 2024.
8. See for example the US government's "Rainwater Harvesting" online tool, which lays out the legality of such harvesting in each state: https://www.energy.gov/femp/rainwater-harvesting-tool (accessed July 3, 2024).
9. It's important to note that this essay is glossing a few aspects of what is in reality a voluminous, two-century-long theoretical tradition—the post-Marxist tradition—that manifests a great deal of disagreement and conflict. For example, the dialectical model I gloss here is not necessarily how all Marxists understand the materialist method.
10. Lincoln Center, "Our Commitment," December 22, 2022, https://www.lincolncenter.org/lincoln-center-at-home/page/our-commitment-to-ongoing-change, accessed July 3, 2024.
11. Willem Marx, "Forget Gas Prices: The Billionaire Club's Run on Cobalt Says Everything About Our Battery-Powered Future," Vanity Fair, April 21,

2022, https://www.vanityfair.com/news/2022/04/the-billionaire-clubs-run-on-cobalt-says-everything-about-our-battery-powered-future; Paul Constant, "Ultrawealthy Americans Want You to Think Their Philanthropy Will Change the World," Business Insider, October 9, 2021, https://www.businessinsider.com/how-ultra-wealthy-americans-use-philanthropy-to-avoid-taxation-2021-10; see the Wikipedia entry on "Artwashing," https://en.wikipedia.org/w/index.php?title=Artwashing&oldid=1223374455; Javier C. Hernández, "A Drone Opera, Brought to You by General Dynamics?" *The New York Times*, May 2, 2023, https://www.nytimes.com/2023/05/02/arts/music/drone-opera-general-dynamics-washington.html; Monica Uszerowicz, "How Some of the World's Biggest Art Patrons Contributed to the Opioid Crisis," Hyperallergic, October 23, 2017), https://hyperallergic.com/406965/how-some-of-the-worlds-biggest-art-patrons-contributed-to-the-opioid-crisis/.

12. David Wilson, "Urban Revitalization on the Upper West Side of Manhattan: An Urban Managerialist Assessment," *Economic Geography* 63, no. 1 (January 1987), 35–47.
13. Karen Chapple, Shannon Jackson, and Anne J. Martin, "Concentrating Creativity: The Planning of Formal and Informal Arts Districts," *City, Culture and Society* 1, no. 4 (December 2010), 225–234. See also Carl Grodach, Nicole Foster, and James Murdoch III, "Gentrification and the Artistic Dividend: The Role of the Arts in Neighborhood Change," *Journal of the American Planning Association* 80, no. 1 (2014): 21–35. Both of these sources demonstrate the centrality of arts institutions to municipal urban renewal schemes, although both focus on whether such schemes are good for the arts rather than on whether they are good for the existing residents of gentrifying areas.
14. Lincoln Center even uses the legacy of the neighborhood it destroyed as part of its branding. See, for example, its October 24, 2023 event "Jazz in San Juan Hill," https://www.lincolncenter.org/series/lincoln-center-presents/jazz-in-san-juan-hill-232.
15. Robinson did not coin the term, but he popularized it his book *Black Marxism: The Making of the Black Radical Tradition* (Zed Press, 1983). See also Robin D. G. Kelley, "What Did Cedric Robinson Mean by Racial Capitalism?" Boston Review, January 12, 2017, https://www.bostonreview.net/articles/robin-d-g-kelley-introduction-race-capitalism-justice/.
16. Jodi Melamed, "Racial Capitalism," *Critical Ethnic Studies* 1, no. 1 (Spring, 2015) 76–85.
17. Olúfẹ́mi O. Táíwò, *Elite Capture: How the Powerful Took Over Identity Politics (And Everything Else)* (Haymarket Books, 2022).

18. The *Grundrisse* refers to an important text in Marxism, the *Grundrisse der Kritik der Politischen Ökonomie* (Foundations of a Critique of Political Economy), an unfinished Marx manuscript written between 1857 and 1858. The *Grundrisse* is particularly meaningful to Marxists because it contains most of the notes and outlines he created while struggling to produce the first volume of *Capital*. In other words, it's a place where you can see his process and his thinking develop.
19. Marianna Ritchey, "Resisting Usefulness: Music and the Political Imagination," *Current Musicology* 108 (Spring 2021), https://journals.library.columbia.edu/index.php/currentmusicology/article/view/7799/4531.
20. If you've been scared off of reading Adorno because of the impression that his work is too elitist, I encourage you to investigate him more deeply. Certainly, he believed European classical music had more moral value than "popular music" under capitalism, but his reasons for holding this belief are extremely complicated and in my opinion more interesting than his detractors often seem to acknowledge. Furthermore, he also diagnosed deep political and moral problems with classical music itself as it developed within European modernity—the "failures" of Beethoven, for example, provide a major source of evidence for Adorno's arguments about how bourgeois liberal humanism contains the seeds of political fascism, and thus helps underscore the argument that Western bourgeois culture itself is a "failure"—hardly a merely elitist argument to make. For a highly readable exploration of Adorno's ideas about popular vs. elite cultural products see Owen Hulatt, "Against Popular Culture," Aeon, February 20, 2018), https://aeon.co/essays/against-guilty-pleasures-adorno-on-the-crimes-of-pop-culture. For a selection of musicological scholarship that attempts a more or less "Marxist" analysis of "the music itself" see: Sumanth Gopinath, "The Problem of the Political in Steve Reich's *Come Out*," in *Sound Commitments: Avant-garde Music and the Sixties*, ed. Robert Adlington (Oxford University Press, 2009), 121–144; Uri Agnon, "How To Do Things With Sounds: New Music as Political Action" (PhD diss., University of Southampton, 2024); Bryan J. Parkhurst and Stephan Hammel, "On Theorizing a 'Properly Marxist' Musical Aesthetics," *International Review of the Aesthetics and Sociology of Music* 48, no. 1 (June, 2017), 33–55; and my book, parts of which attempt to analyze the music of Mason Bates and some of the "indie classical" composers based in Brooklyn, NY, *Composing Capital: Classical Music in the Neoliberal Era* (University of Chicago Press, 2019).

THE THING ITSELF

Karl Marx, *Capital: A Critique of Political Economy, Volume 1.* (Most English readers use the Penguin Classics edition—that's the one that cited page numbers in English-language scholarship will often refer to, so it's a nice one to use.) You can also read *Capital* free of charge online at https://www.marxists.org/archive/marx/works/1867-c1/, and there's an audiobook version as well (https://www.marxists.org/audiobooks/archive/marx-engels/capital-vol1/).

David Harvey, *A Companion to Marx's* Capital (Verso, 2018). Harvey's lifetime's work introducing newcomers to Marx is a beautiful example of radical pedagogy (and anyone who's read him will no doubt see many of his formulations in the essay I've just written). Not only does he write these "companion" books that you can read alongside Marx's various writings, he also teaches free video courses you can watch while reading (https://davidharvey.org/2019/02/reading-marxs-capital-vol-1-2019-class-1-introduction/).

Karl Marx and Friedrich Engels, *The Communist Manifesto* (if you want to start with a quick and readable description of what's wrong with capitalism and what life might look like if it were destroyed). Online at https://www.marxists.org/archive/marx/works/download/pdf/Manifesto.pdf.

MARXIST/MATERIALIST APPROACHES TO MUSIC

Bryan J. Parkhurst, "Music, Art, and Kinds of Use Values," *Critique* 48, no. 2–3 (2020). Parkhurst uses Marxist arguments about the labor theory of value to explore what kind of product music is, as well as what constitutes its value as a commodity under capitalism.

Eric Drott, *Streaming Music, Streaming Capital* (Duke University Press, 2024). Drott writes about Spotify and other online streaming platforms from a Marxist perspective.

Kyle Devine, *Decomposed: The Political Ecology of Music* (MIT Press, 2019). A materialist history of popular music. Devine moves away from the idealist way of talking about music history and actually digs into the material reality of recordings, examining the record industry's reliance on fossil fuels and other natural and human resources.

Timothy Taylor, *Music and Capitalism: A History of the Present* (University of Chicago Press, 2015). Explores US "commercial music" across the twentieth century in order to demonstrate some of the profound ways it has been shaped by the capitalist system.

Tamara Levitz, "The Musicological Elite," *Current Musicology* 102 (2018). Levitz seeks to tell a materialist story of the founding of the American Musicological Society (AMS). Much like my story about Lincoln Center, she uncovers the concrete, real-world goals the AMS was founded on, and contrasts these with the idealistic statements about itself the AMS publicizes today, particularly with regard to goals of diversification or decolonization.

Marianna Ritchey, "Resisting Usefulness: Music and the Political Imagination," *Current Musicology* 108 (Summer 2021). Mentioned above.

Kirsten L. Speyer Carithers, "Music History as Labor History: Rethinking 'Work' in Musicology," *Journal of Music History Pedagogy* 12, no. 1 (2022): 68–90.

John Pippen, "Hope, Labour and Privilege in American New Music," in *Music as Labour: Inequalities and Activism in the Past and Present*, edited by Dagmar Abfalter and Rosa Reitsamer (Routledge: 2022), 81–96. See also Pippen's essay "Music and/as Work" in this issue of *Open Access Musicology*. Both Pippen and Carithers are musicologists who try to nail down what the labor of music or music history is. What is the work of these fields? How do we create products and how does this labor get exploited by capitalists? Music is a slippery subject for such investigations, and Carithers and Pippen are showing an exciting new way forward in this regard.

POST-MARXIST DEVELOPMENTS CONCERNING RACE AND GENDER AND LAND DISPOSSESSION

Cedric Robinson, *Black Marxism: The Making of the Black Radical Tradition* (Zed Press, 1983).

Silvia Federici, *Caliban and the Witch: Women, the Body, and Primitive Accumulation* (Autonomedia, 2004).

Holly Lewis, *The Politics of Everybody: Feminism, Queer Theory, and Marxism at the Intersection* (Zed Books, 2016).

Jodi Melamed, "Racial Capitalism," *Critical Ethnic Studies* 1, no. 1 (Spring 2015) 76–85.

Vanessa Wills, "What Could It Mean to Say, 'Capitalism Causes Sexism and Racism?'," *Philosophical Topics* 46, no. 2 (Fall 2018) 229–246.

Keeanga-Yamahtta Taylor, *Race for Profit: How Banks and the Real Estate Industry Undermined Black Homeownership* (University of North Carolina Press, 2019).

Susan Koshy, Lisa Marie Cacho, Jodi A. Byrd, and Brian Jordan Jefferson, eds., *Colonial Racial Capitalism* (Duke University Press, 2022).

Olúfẹ́mi O. Táíwò, *Elite Capture: How the Powerful Took Over Identity Politics (And Everything Else)* (Haymarket Books, 2022).

CHAPTER FIVE

MUSIC AND/AS WORK

John R. Pippen

This article originated in part from my experiences with thinking about music as a form of work. Musicology, and musical scholarship in general, has been very inconsistent in how it approaches issues of labor. My own graduate writing about contemporary classical musicians in Chicago demonstrates this inconsistency, and I eventually realized that musicians themselves can be very confusing when they apply the concept of work to their music-making. Looking back, I now see how contradictory understandings of music manifested in my own life. As an aspiring classical musician during my undergraduate education, I met many people who thought a person couldn't earn a living in music and that a degree in music was a waste of time. And yet those same people would profess a deep passion for the music they loved. These characterizations took a long time for me to fully and consciously articulate, but the disconnect between how people valued music and how they disparaged the idea of working in music always bothered me. During my playing years, I spent thousands of hours learning music, practicing different techniques, watching videos of myself playing, taking lessons, playing juries, and auditioning for all manner of things. Music for me was in no uncertain terms highly legitimate work. Having my efforts judged intrinsically wasteful was deeply frustrating. I grew to reject the notion that my love for music justified the low pay I received for my work. Extending that to others, I believe that loving what they do does not mean that musicians should earn less or endure more precarity than any other occupation. I hope this article will provide a way for us to interrogate how we assign value to music, music-making, and musicians. So, I write here a version of an article I wish I could have found as an undergrad.

This article investigates how and when music is defined as "work." There is no objective definition of work. Rather, I treat work as a discursive concept shaped by the cultural logics of a given society. "Work" and its frequent synonym "labor" have undergone many changing definitions over time. Even in a given historical setting, people have had intense disagreements about what does and does not count as work. From this, scholars of the history of words have noted that "work itself has been a contested concept."[1] Some have attempted deeper theoretical distinctions between work and labor, but these efforts generally faltered because they fail to centralize the contested nature of the terms and the social relationships they imply.[2]

As philosopher Kathi Weeks argues, the designation of certain activities as work have had important implications in the twentieth and twenty-first centuries.[3] A good example of this contestation can be seen in debates about labor done in the home, "housework" such as laundry, dishwashing, meal preparation, and childcare. Many economists writing in the early twentieth century described these activities as "women's work" in disparaging terms, to the effect that, even when a man did them, they were lower status than some other work seen as properly male. Feminists, in contrast, argued that activities done in the home were important work because the people engaged in it (usually understood to be women) supported the paid labor of the worker (usually understood to be a man) who left the home. If no one fed, cared for, bought clothes for, or entertained the worker, "he" would be unable to be productive at his place of employment. Feminists argued that what was taken as a natural set of roles, a male "breadwinner" and a female "homemaker," was in fact the result of social relationships subject to historical change. They pointed out that earlier economic systems made very different distinctions between men's and women's activities.[4] Accounting for these types of debates draws attention to the ways that the discourse of work interacts with other discourses such as gender.

In general, I focus on capitalist social systems because, in the current era, capitalism is the dominant system shaping notions of work. Nearly all the world's people must negotiate aspects of capitalism throughout their lives. This negotiation manifests as the compulsion to find work in order to buy what is needed to sustain life, a defining characteristic of a capitalist society.[5] A person in a capitalist society need not be employed in a for-profit enterprise in order to earn the money required to secure livelihood. They can work in a not-for-profit endeavor, such as public teaching, grant writing, or in music-making for a church. However, these activities are, as leading Marxist scholar Nancy Fraser has argued, still shaped by the general social prioritization of capitalist accumulation.[6] Public teaching, for example, in the United States is funded by property taxes, which are assessed according to the imagined value of a home. In nonprofit sectors, organizations rely on sales to and donations from people who are often members of upper classes or who are themselves capitalists. Returning to music, this means that even musicians who earn their living teaching at a school will be affected by capitalist logics of accumulation. Their classroom budgets are ultimately determined, in part, by the relative value of homes, and they often have to solicit donations and apply for grants in order to fund music programs. Teachers also do not make everything they need for life. They do not sew their clothes, build their instruments, write their sheet music, or grow their own food. Rather, they earn a wage by selling their labor power (in this case music teaching), and then exchange those wages for needed commodities. The commodity form is intrinsic to capitalist production, shapes the social relations of people in capitalist societies, and deeply impacts how people interact with the world. Labor is itself another commodity form in capitalism, a fact marked by Marx with the phrase "labor power."

How do these facts of life manifest in music? In work? What might music *at* people's places of work be or do? What about music *as* work? To answer these questions, we should consider the ways people discursively frame music and work. Understanding work as a material aspect of people's lives and as discourse helps demonstrate the logics of activities, including musical activities. These can include how people have fun, how they earn wages, accrue social favors, accumulate profits, exploit each other, and how they construct gender, and race.[7] I divide my article into three parts. First, I examine music *at* work. Drawing on the work of sociologists, I summarize the ways music has structured work, how it came to be separate from work, and how it has been reintegrated into workplaces. Capitalist forms of production separated work from leisure in new ways, and music came to be widely treated as a form of leisure during the nineteenth century. In the second section, I consider music *as* work through three types of working relationships that have impacted music around the world: patronage, guilds (and by extension unions), and independent work. Much of my historicization here draws explicitly on the recent work of Stephan Hammel as well as older sources.[8] Casting music as leisure has had enduring consequences to how we value (or disparage) music as a form of labor. In a final section, I suggest questions for discussion with relevant sources. By adopting a critical orientation to work, we can see that music is not, in fact, a simple form of leisure that soothes our beleaguered minds. Rather, music emerges as a necessary aspect of human life that has been deeply affected by changing social relationships of production. Considered together, music and work demonstrate how people experience crucial parts of their lives and how they think of each other.

MUSIC *AT* WORK

As several scholars have demonstrated, people have called music-making both leisure and work.[9] This division rose in large part because of the changes in labor associated with nineteenth-century industrial capitalism. Precapitalist modes of production often used music in workplaces extensively. Music was often a way to time the movements of work. Sea shanties, for example, were used to time the collaborative labor required to haul sails and perform other activities.[10] With the rise of capitalism, however, many workers lost the ability to coordinate their labor through music. Instead, industrial machinery, controlled by owners, dictated the flow of work. Music *at* work, then, was a part of people's relationships and how they coordinated their activities. Singing, a feature of labor for hundreds of years prior to industrial capitalism, was often forbidden in new industrial settings, and workers who sang, whistled, or made other unapproved sounds at work were fined. Just as work was increasingly an activity imagined to be performed outside the home, so too was music relegated to the realm of leisure. This development paralleled a change in audience behavior at concerts. Early in nineteenth-century Europe, audiences were highly interactive with onstage performers, often demanding to hear popular tunes. Later, however, composers demanded—and achieved—silence so that audiences could concentrate on musical works.[11]

Sociologist Marek Korczynski's work usefully demonstrates how music and work are deeply intertwined in each other.[12] Changes in one often resulted in changes of the other. He historicizes music at work into three epochs: preindustrial, which I described above; industrial; and postindustrial. Lest we be overly tidy in our histories of music at work, Korczynski warns, "No attempt is made to put strict dates to these periods, as the uneven nature of industrialization and postindustrialization make such efforts problematic."[13] Put another way, older forms of working often exist alongside newer ones. Methods of working and of assembling goods have spread unevenly around the world, affecting different industries in different ways. It took a long time, for example, for industrial modes of production to replace older methods of assembly and some older forms of production continue to exist.[14] Korczynski's approach usefully allows for, in his words, the "historically messy" changes in labor over time.[15] It also provides greater clarity for examining the social relationships of specific workplaces.

Though industrial capitalist workplaces restricted sound early on, they gradually embraced the use of music at work. This was done for two reasons. First, many workers in industrial settings found the repetitive motions of their jobs boring. Music provided an escape from the drudgery of work. This reinforced the view of music as a form of leisure. Music provided a way for people to experience time in relationship to entertaining sounds, as opposed to through the highly regulated movements of their jobs. Second, in contrast with early industrial models that opposed sound at work, later models used music to enhance the output of workers. Thus, for example, in the twentieth century muzak was marketed as a way to increase productivity.[16] Muzak consisted of arrangements of popular tunes into somehow "calmer" versions. By using music that people found nostalgic, (by manipulating tempi, timbre, and often eliminating lyrics) managers used music to keep workers productive during times when their energy flagged. In addition to other boss-approved musics, muzak kept workers docile, obedient to their managers and the goals of capitalists.[17]

More recently, changes in music technology have enabled workers to have more control over music in some workplaces. Portable music devices from the Walkman to the smartphone have allowed people to create their own soundtracks for work. However, such technologies are not always equally available to all people. As Korczynski's ethnographic research in a mini-blinds factory demonstrates, employers still restrict workers' musical listening.[18] Music in these settings can continue to provide a sense of escape from the boredom of repetitive labor, but it can also amplify drudgery. Workers in the factory Korczynski studied could choose between only two music radio stations. After hours on of hearing the same songs cycled through on these two stations, workers in his study described their fatigue at hearing the same popular songs over and over again. Such experiences made work worse by accentuating the lack of control workers had over their jobs.

As this research demonstrates, music has much to teach us about what work is and how people think about it. The two can be mutually constitutive of each other, as in the case of work songs in preindustrial settings.

It can also demonstrate how music seems to function as a site of leisure or escape from work. The question of who controls music in the workplace reveals power arrangements within single workplaces and across job hierarchies. What about, then, music *as* work?

MUSIC *AS* WORK

Just as music *at* work demonstrates how people understand one another, their activities, and themselves, so too does studying music *as* work. In this section, I will consider three general types of social relationships common to musicians: patron-based relationships, old European guilds, and the rise of independent musicians under capitalism. Each of these relationships provides researchers with a way of understanding how music and musicians are valued, how people define work, and how socio-musical relationships change over time. Finally, all these types of relationships have existed alongside one another and persist, in various ways, into the present.[19] This section provides a historically informed consideration of the kinds of social relationships one may encounter in musical labor.

Patronage

One of the most common types of musical labor relationships is patronage. Musicians around the world have, throughout history, worked in the employ of a single patron or groups of patrons. For much of European history, musicians often worked in patronage relationships with specific aristocrats, churches (especially large cathedrals), and with educational institutions. Often when I teach patronage, students assume such positions were highly exploitative or unfair. This mischaracterizes the issue. Musicologist Deborah Rohr has argued that patronage with aristocrats, churches, and universities granted musical work a higher status than it might otherwise have enjoyed.[20] It had a respected canon of theoretical knowledge, recognition by ruling classes and powerful institutions, and high social value because of music's roles in public secular and sacred ceremonies. Music was also respected because it was part of the liberal arts, a canon of knowledge required of any gentleman or lady. In many of these arrangements, the musician received payment both in money and "in kind," or in goods and services. For example, Joseph Haydn (1732–1809) was paid for his musical services to the Estehązy family both in money and in the materials needed to live, such as firewood, housing, board, and clothing.[21] Musicians in such relationships usually did not own the music they created, though in practice many could profit from it either through direct payment (if permitted by the patron) or through the increase in reputation that such compositions might afford. Most canonized classical composers had the support of multiple patrons at different times in their lives, and much of the music that defines classical music, from Beethoven's symphonies to Wagner's operas, would not exist without the financial support of wealthy patrons.

Musical positions funded by wealthy patrons or institutions were often considered prestigious, but musicians in general were not an especially respected group. As Walter Salmen argued, we ought not conflate the status of music with that of the musicians who produced it.[22] Though music has been a major aspect of human life, it has not necessarily afforded autonomy to musicians in their creative endeavors. That music could be so crucial to humanity but musicians less so is one of the enduring contradictions of musical work. Studying patronage, then, is both a study in the working relationships that shape music and the ways that elites use music in *their* social lives. As musicologist Paul Merkley emphasizes, studying patronage is a way to map out the social networks that create specific musical practices or works and that shape the lives of all involved.[23]

Patronage relationships persist into the present. Today, many musicians continue to foster close connections with wealthy donors and elite institutions. Institutions such as the British Broadcasting Corporation, the French *Institut de recherche et coordination acoustique/musique*, and the National Endowment for the Arts provide more modern examples of patronage (though filtered through the logics of capitalist societies more generally).[24] These institutions have patronized music not simply out of a love of the arts, but because the arts provide a way to circulate prestige and to facilitate close relationships among powerful elites. These cases also demonstrate the persistence of older precapitalist forms of production and can help nuance our understanding of the different kinds of working relationships that musicians have.

Guilds

Prior to the rise of capitalism, many musicians organized themselves into city-based work collectives called guilds. Guild organizations can be found throughout history in many different settings, typically as part of a large society that regularly featured musical performances, especially performances associated with ruling classes. The conditions and privileges afforded specific guilds could vary considerably. They were also subject to change. A new ruler could come to power and abolish established guild relationships because that ruler already had their own group of musicians.

In general, guilds were part of a broader labor strategy whereby relatively low status workers could improve their material conditions and prospects. Understood as a social relationship between employers and employed, guilds illustrate a struggle to increase the social standing of musical work and the status of those who practiced it. Active in Europe from around the twelfth century to the nineteenth century, guilds generally had two goals.[25] First, they sought to establish control over who was allowed to perform music in specific settings. This monopoly over labor was common among other types of guilds. Bakers, for example, would create guilds that prohibited non-guild makers from selling bread in a given city. Medieval and Renaissance musicians secured this control over labor by pledging themselves to a given ruler or municipal authority, an arrangement that bound the musicians to the systems of honor associated with ruling classes. This granted guild musicians a better social standing than was afforded independent touring musicians (a group often considered dishonorable). Second, guilds gave considerable control over the details of musical work to musicians themselves. Prospective guild members had to present letters that attested to their trustworthiness, skill, and legitimate birth. In order to control access to the skills required to perform, guild musicians were forbidden from teaching non-guild members, had to pay into collective funds, and had to adhere to rules governing the hierarchy of players. In return, they received certain rights (such as the right to receive Holy Communion), better pay, access to health care, pensions, benevolence funds, and more stable work conditions.

Most guilds saw their power decline in the 1700s and many lost their privileges in the 1790s and 1800s. However, they demonstrate a few important and enduring aspects of musical labor. First, musicians have long sought to align themselves with ruling classes as part of a struggle for recognition, respect, and remuneration. Contemporary musicians continue to struggle for these, even when they are idealized as artists. Second, collective efforts have often successfully improved the lives of musicians. Imagine if, upon the completion of your musical training and admission to a guild, you were guaranteed health care, a pension, and access to regular predictable musical work (at least until some new ruler came to power). Many contemporary musicians would see these as major privileges! These types of privileges have figured prominently in musical unionizing.

Independent Musicians

The rise of independent musicians (those working outside of patronage or guild systems) coincided with the spread of industrial capitalism and the growth of cities from the seventeenth to the nineteenth centuries. Though some cities had been large cultural centers for centuries, prior to the nineteenth century most were relatively small, and the majority of the world's population lived in rural settings. The transition to capitalist economic systems was gradual and saw many rural farmers forced off their land and compelled to work in cities or face destitution.[26] There was also an increase in mercantilism and the flow of goods from around the world. Throughout the seventeenth century, independent merchants and independent workers were increasingly tolerated and even respected.[27] They were bolstered in part by the writings of Enlightenment philosophers such as Adam Smith who idealized capitalist markets as providing paths to individual freedom. This shift, as explained above, saw changes in how musicians used music as a way to regulate the flow of labor. It also led to an increase in the demand for music in large and growing cities, a change documented by historians such as Peter Gay, James H. Johnson, and William Weber.[28] Musicologist Daniel Cavicchi has demonstrated how people in nineteenth century United States were shocked by the sounds of cities and overwhelmed by the variety of musical performances they provided.[29] Musicians took advantage of these changes by organizing their own concerts, often of music they had written themselves. Previously considered low status, virtuosos who traveled from town to town became more esteemed. By the time Ludwig van Beethoven (1770–1827) moved to Vienna in 1792, such virtuosity was in high demand, especially within the wealthy salons of the city's aristocrats.[30]

While this change is important to highlight, it can obscure the endurance of older forms of working relationships. Many musicians worked in a mixture of patronage, short-term contracts, or one-time services. Notably, however, independent work was increasingly idealized in the nineteenth century (an idealization that persists into the present). Musicians, including many performers, often described themselves not simply as workers selling their skills for money, but as "artists" who transcended both the marketplace and the demands of patrons. This can be seen most clearly in the writings of the canonized Romantic composers such as Robert Schumann (1810–1856), Hector Berlioz (1803–1869), and Richard Wagner (1813–1883).[31] As "free" artists, musicians could escape the demands of wealthy patrons and ignore the demands of the public.[32] Though Wagner and piano virtuoso Franz Liszt (1811–1886) actually relied upon the patronage of wealthy aristocrats, they were afforded much more freedom than was common for patronage-supported musicians in previous eras. Understood as artists, these musicians reinforced the changes in music's social function. Where it had once been integrated into people's everyday work, music was increasingly separate from work, as described above. Most importantly, music gradually came to be understood as a specialized activity for especially "musical" people. Since that time, musicians around the world have often had to negotiate tensions between music as work and music as artistry.

An enduring challenge to the study of music *as* work is how it has frequently been treated as somehow not work, even when it is the result of the cultivation of years of training and sold for money. The contradiction between musicians as workers and as artists persisted with musicians' unionizing efforts.[33] In large part, musicians in the early twentieth century were more likely to embrace the label of "worker" as it facilitated successful unionizing.[34] Such campaigns led to higher wages, rules for working conditions, and even pensions. In this way, they paralleled the strategies of the old guilds. Unionizing even slowed the spread of recorded sound. The American Federation of Musicians (AFM), led by President James Patrillo, fought to prohibit the use of records in place of live musicians, eventually winning major concessions from the record companies and radio stations in the 1940s.[35] In the latter half of the century, however, most AFM musicians moved away from the embrace of the worker identity. This was motivated in part by the union itself, who rejected some forms of popular music on the basis of racist and classist values. It was also motivated by record companies seeking to commodify new trends in music. These companies increasingly described musicians with record contracts as "recording musicians." This designation set them apart from other "side players" who played for a record but were not considered the main attraction.[36] This was a useful strategy not so much for the performers, but for the studios that benefited from pay hierarchies.

As we can see, treating music *as* work poses many complications. I would like to make a final argument to help us approach such cases. In many situations it would be accurate to describe musicians, especially when they are legally classified as recording artists, as enjoying a status higher than that of many working people. Many people understand music as a somehow more fulfilling or fun activity when compared with all sorts of other jobs. Record companies, marketing professionals, and musicians themselves frequently emphasize the creativity of music, implicitly contrasting it with the "normal" work of "normal" people. However, I argue that just because an activity is fun does not make it *not* work. Earning a living from music usually requires that people acquire skills over years, build up networks, and accept engagements that they would prefer to decline. What's more, the overwhelming majority of people in capitalist societies must work in order to earn enough money to buy what they need to live. As Matt Stahl has argued, recording artists remain workers because they live in a capitalist society that *requires* most people to work.[37] Thus, when considering whether an activity qualifies as work we should ask whether this activity is part of a broader social compulsion toward work. The compulsion to work, after all, would inform the individual musician's understanding of their activity. Surely being a successful recording artist is an enviable position, but that evaluation is made in consideration of other possible occupations. Music as work seems ideal because it implicitly calls to mind other somehow worse possibilities for earning a living. And yet, even if musical labor is especially fun or fulfilling, the fact remains that musicians sell their labor power for money needed to survive. They work.

DISCUSSION QUESTIONS

Here are a few discussion questions to help guide your consideration of music and work. I have included one or two useful sources directly related to each question.

1. Have you ever worked in a context where music was playing but you had no control over it? Did you like that? Did your coworkers?

   - Korczynski, Marek. *Songs of the Factory: Pop Music, Culture, and Resistance.* Cornell University Press, 2014.

2. If you play or sing for money do you think of yourself as an artist or as a worker? Does your understanding of your identity change from context to context?

    - McLeod, Bruce A. *Club Date Musicians: Playing the New York Party Circuit.* University of Illinois Press, 1993.
    - Taylor, Timothy D. *Working Musicians: Labor and Creativity in Film and Television Production.* Duke University Press, 2023.

3. What arguments have you heard about artists who claim that they are controlled and dominated by their record companies? Do those artists' claims seem credible? Why or why not? What about when some artists charge other artists with appropriating their work without crediting or compensating them?

    - Feld, Steven. "Pygmy Pop. A Genealogy of Schizophonic Mimesis." *Yearbook for Traditional Music* 28 (1996): 1–35.
    - Samples, Mark C. "Timbre and Legal Likeness: The Case of Tom Waits." In *The Relentless Pursuit of Tone: Timbre in Popular Music*, edited by Robert Wallace Fink, Melinda Latour, and Zachary Wallmark, 119–40. Oxford University Press, 2018.

4. Do you pay to go to concerts? Do you buy recordings? Sheet music? Do you support performers or composers via Patreon or other crowdfunding initiatives? Do you pay for streaming? Do you download without paying? Are you getting your money's worth? Are the performers entitled to a share?

    - Eriksson, Maria, Rasmus Fleischer, Anna Johansson, Pelle Snickars, and Patrick Vonderau. *Spotify Teardown: Inside the Black Box of Streaming Music.* MIT Press, 2019.

5. Is there value in private individuals and corporations sponsoring the arts? Should governments fund the arts? Can you think of an example when your work or the work of someone you knew was funded through patronage?

    - Merkley, Paul A., ed. *Music and Patronage*. Ashgate, 2012.

NOTES

1. Tony Bennett, Lawrence Grossberg, and Meaghan Morris, eds., *New Keywords: A Revised Vocabulary of Culture and Society* (Blackwell, 2005), 375.
2. Some scholars make distinctions between "work" and "labor," in part because of the histories of these particular words. I will use them interchangeably in this article. For a treatment that seeks to parse work from labor, see Hannah Arendt, *The Human Condition*, 2nd ed. (University of Chicago Press, 1998). Raymond Williams wrote a most useful book for such considerations. See Colin MacCabe and Holly Yanacek, *Keywords for Today: A 21st Century Vocabulary* (Oxford University Press, 2018).
3. Kathi Weeks, *The Problem with Work: Feminism, Marxism, Antiwork Politics, and Postwork Imaginaries* (Duke University Press, 2011).
4. Andrea Komlosy, *Work: The Last 1,000 Years*, trans. Loren Balhorn and Jacob K. Watson (Verso, 2018); Silvia Federici, *Caliban and the Witch: Women, the Body and Primitive Accumulation* (Autonomedia, 2004).
5. Karl Marx described the naturalization of this social reality as intrinsic to modern capitalism. Karl Marx, *Capital: A Critique of Political Economy, Volume 1*, trans. Ben Fowkes (Penguin Books in association with New Left Review, 1990). Søren Mau develops this concept to demonstrate how capitalism persists even while it creates all sorts of crises. Søren Mads Mau, *Mute Compulsion: A Marxist Theory of the Economic Power of Capital* (Verso, 2023).
6. Nancy Fraser, "Behind Marx's Hidden Abode: For an Expanded Conception of Capitalism," *New Left Review* no. 86 (March/April 2014): 55–72.
7. For more theoretical discussion of these issues in music, see Matt Stahl, "Popular Musical Labor in North America," in *The Sage Handbook of Popular Music*, ed. Andy Bennett and Steve Waksman, 135–53 (Sage, 2015). Matt Stahl, "Primitive Accumulation, the Social Common, and the Contractual Lockdown of Recording Artists at the Threshold of Digitalization," *Ephemera: Theory and Politics in Organization* 10, no. 3/4 (2010): 337–55; Bennett et al., *New Keywords*.
8. Stephan Hammel, *Toward a Materialist Conception of Music History* (Brill, 2025).
9. Useful nuances of this issue have been explored by several scholars. See Karl Hagstrom Miller, "Working Musicians: Exploring the Rhetorical Ties between Musical Labour and Leisure," *Leisure Studies* 27, no. 4 (2008): 427–41; Mike Jones, "The Music Industry as Workplace: An Approach to Analysis," in *Cultural Work: Understanding the Cultural Industries*, ed. Andrew Beck, 147–56 (Taylor & Francis, 2002); Matt Stahl, *Unfree Masters: Popular Music and the Politics of Work* (Duke University Press, 2013).

10. A. L. Lloyd, *Folk Song in England* (International Publishers, 1967); Marek Korczynski, "Music at Work: Towards a Historical Overview," *Folk Music Journal* 8, no. 3 (2003): 314–34.
11. Lawrence W. Levine, *Highbrow/Lowbrow: The Emergence of Cultural Hierarchy in America* (Harvard University Press, 1988); Daniel Cavicchi, *Listening and Longing: Music Lovers in the Age of Barnum* (Wesleyan University Press, 2011); Christian Thorau and Hansjakob Ziemer, eds., *The Oxford Handbook of Music Listening in the 19th and 20th Centuries* (Oxford University Press, 2019).
12. Korczynski, "Music at Work"; Craig Prichard, Marek Korczynski, and Michael Elmes, "Music at Work: An Introduction," *Group & Organization Management* 32, no. 1 (2007): 4–21, https://doi.org/10.1177/1059601106294485; Marek Korczynski, Michael Pickering, and Emma Robertson, eds., *Rhythms of Labour: Music at Work in Britain* (Cambridge University Press, 2013).
13. Korczynski, "Music at Work," 316.
14. Komlosy, *Work*.
15. Korczynski, "Music at Work," 316.
16. Kit Hughes, *Television at Work: Industrial Media and American Labor* (Oxford University Press, 2020).
17. For a fascinating case study of workplace singing at IBM, see Amal El-Sawad and Marek Korczynski, "Management and Music: The Exceptional Case of the IBM Songbook," *Group & Organization Management* 32, no. 1 (2007): 79–108, https://doi.org/10.1177/1059601106294488.
18. Marek Korczynski, *Songs of the Factory: Pop Music, Culture, and Resistance* (Cornell University Press, 2014).
19. Wiliam Weber, "The Musician as Entrepreneur and Opportunist, 1700–1914," in *The Musician as Entrepreneur, 1700–1914: Managers, Charlatans, and Idealists*, ed. William Weber, 3–24 (Indiana University Press, 2004).
20. Deborah Rohr, *The Careers and Social Status of British Musicians, 1750–1850: A Profession of Artisans* (Cambridge University Press, 2001).
21. Piero Weiss and Richard Taruskin, editors, "Haydn's Duties in the Service of Prince Esterházy," in *Music in the Western World: A History in Documents*, ed. Piero Weiss and Richard Taruskin, 252–54 (Thomson/Schirmer, 2008).
22. Walter Salmen, "The Social Status of the Musician in the Middle Ages," in *The Social Status of the Professional Musician from the Middle Ages to the 19th Century*, ed. Walter Salmen, Herbert Kaufman, and Barbara Reisner, 1–30 (Pendragon Press, 1983).
23. Paul A. Merkley, ed., *Music and Patronage* (Ashgate, 2012). Merkley's book pulls together many case studies of patronage from all over the world.

24. Jennifer Doctor, *The BBC and Ultra-Modern Music, 1922–1936: Shaping a Nation's Tastes*, Music in the Twentieth Century, (Cambridge University Press, 1999); Georgina Born, *Rationalizing Culture: IRCAM, Boulez, and the Institutionalization of the Musical Avant-Garde* (University of California Press, 1995); Donna M. Binkiewicz, *Federalizing the Muse: United States Arts Policy and the National Endowment for the Arts, 1965–1980* (University of North Carolina Press, 2004).
25. Much of this section is drawn from the entry for "Guilds" in Grove Music Online. It contains a timeline useful for further research. See Heinrich W. Schwab, "Guilds," *Grove Music Online* (2001), https://doi.org/10.1093/gmo/9781561592630.article.11976.
26. This process was described by eighteenth century political economists as "primitive accumulation," a term Marx famously mocked in the final section of *Capital*. For a modern explanation of Marx's historicization, see Hadas Thier, *A People's Guide to Capitalism: An Introduction to Marxist Economics* (Haymarket Press, 2020). For an extension of Marx's ideas to more recent aspects of capitalism, see David Harvey, "The 'New' Imperialism: Accumulation by Dispossession," *Socialist Register* 40 (2004): 63–87; Jim Glassman, "Primitive Accumulation, Accumulation by Dispossession, Accumulation by 'Extra-Economic' Means," *Progress in Human Geography* 30, no. 5 (2006): 608–25, https://doi.org/10.1177/0309132506070172. For an application of primitive accumulation to music, see Stahl, "Primitive Accumulation."
27. Weber, "The Musician as Entrepreneur."
28. Peter Gay, *The Bourgeois Experience: Victoria to Freud* (Oxford University Press, 1984); James H. Johnson, *Listening in Paris: A Cultural History* (University of California Press, 1995); William Weber, *The Great Transformation of Musical Taste: Concert Programming from Haydn to Brahms* (Cambridge University Press, 2008).
29. Cavicchi, *Listening and Longing*.
30. DeNora Tia, *Beethoven and the Construction of Genius: Musical Politics in Vienna, 1792–1803* (University of California Press, 1995).
31. Alexander Stefaniak, *Schumann's Virtuosity: Criticism, Composition, and Performance in Nineteenth-Century Germany* (Indiana University Press, 2016); Nicholas Vazsonyi, *Richard Wagner: Self-Promotion and the Making of a Brand* (Cambridge University Press, 2010).
32. Lydia Goehr's discussion of these trends is most useful to engaging changes in how people framed music as art. See Chapter 8 in Lydia Goehr, *The Imaginary Museum of Musical Works: An Essay in the Philosophy of Music*, rev. ed. (Oxford University Press, 2007).

33. James P. Kraft, *Stage to Studio: Musicians and the Sound Revolution, 1890–1950* (Johns Hopkins University Press, 1996).
34. Stahl, "Popular Musical Labor in North America."
35. Michael James Roberts, *Tell Tchaikovsky the News: Rock'n'Roll, the Labor Question, and the Musicians' Union, 1942–1968* (Duke University Press, 2014).
36. Stahl, "Popular Musical Labor in North America."
37. Stahl, "Popular Musical Labor in North America."

CHAPTER SIX

DANGEROUS UNDERTAKINGS

Judicial Copyright Opinions as Music Criticism

Katherine M. Leo

One of my goals as an academic and forensic musicologist is to bridge disciplinary gaps between music and law. What can I offer law as a musicologist? How can my legal training inform, or even expand, musicology? There are many parallels in the kinds of questions that legal specialists and musicologists ask, in part because both disciplines are interested in understanding the nature of musical creativity. Yet specialists in each discipline typically apply different methods and resources to these inquiries.

Legal questions pertaining to specific musical works are typically addressed at common law through lawsuits. Judicial opinions that resolve these cases are an essential part of my work. More than simply public legal records that document facts and outcomes, these opinions can, and should, be viewed as historical records. They offer windows into the ways that judges as individuals and public servants interpret laws. When these opinions are considered in relation to one another, readers can trace the development of legal philosophy surrounding concepts of similarity or the role of musical analysis in legal decision-making processes. By reading these judicial opinions through multiple lenses—not only legal but also historical and, indeed, musicological—they can be interpreted as a kind of music criticism. This fascinating phenomenon is made troubling, however, by contravening law that prohibits judges' aesthetic valuations of copyrightable works.

This essay is part of my effort to frame judicial opinions for a cross-disciplinary audience, with the goal here of inspiring investigation of judicial aesthetics while furthering dialogues about the regulation of musical works as intellectual property. Footnoted cases have hyperlinks to open-access judicial opinions for further reading alongside resources that explain fundamental concepts in law and forensic musicology. Music copyright law continues to evolve, so my hope is that readers will use this essay as a foundation for examining not only the historic opinions that I have included here, but also the most recent cases unfolding as they read.

Judges in federal music copyright lawsuits preside over courtroom discourse on music as intellectual property. Their decisions as to the outcome of each case resolve interrelated legal matters, such as authorship, originality, and similarity. This task is one legally presumed to be impartial, guided by a body of laws intended to inform and regulate judicial interpretation. Since the 1903 lawsuit of *Bleistein v. Donaldson Lithographing Co.*, copyright laws have limited the influence that aesthetic judgments can, and should, have on infringement proceedings. Yet over a century of judicial opinions suggests that judges' musical critiques, known to the *Bleistein* court as "dangerous undertaking[s]," seem unavoidable.

In light of this legal conundrum, the present essay frames judicial opinions as music criticism. After an overview of the US legal system, it contextualizes a selection of twentieth- and twenty-first-century copyright infringement cases according to their contemporaneous public and judicial musical tastes. It identifies judicial ambivalence toward the *Bleistein* ruling, shown in judges' word choice and value statements about the musical works in each case that often reveal enduring elitism surrounding commercial popular music. These decisions therefore raise questions about the impact that such aesthetic evaluations might have on case outcomes. While a comprehensive analysis of opinions, aesthetic matters, cultural influences, and legal issues is beyond the scope of this essay, it begins to map a cross-disciplinary terrain of judicial music aesthetics and calls for further dialogue about practical ways to mitigate the "dangerous undertaking" of federal music copyright litigation.

JUDICIAL OPINIONS IN US FEDERAL LAW

The US judiciary is part of a common law system: the legislative branch crafts statutes that are then interpreted by the judicial branch through the litigation process. Written decisions rendered by judges determine the outcome of each lawsuit by interpreting existing laws, both relevant statutes and prior precedential decisions, and applying them to the individual facts of each lawsuit. Judicial opinions, therefore, are supposed to clarify legal uncertainties. As common law, these decisions constitute the determination of a court, which has binding—or at least persuasive—authority, depending on the jurisdiction; and they are enforceable unless or until they are overturned by a new statute or a later opinion.[1] The evolution of federal common law therefore shapes, and is shaped by, a cumulating body of judicial opinions. Most of these documents are treated as part of public record and therefore widely accessible online and in print.

Although each case, its parties, and the presiding judge(s) are different, judges tend to draft their opinions according to common organizational patterns. One presiding judge usually writes an opinion for each district court-level case; appeals of those decisions to appellate circuit courts are usually heard by three-judge panels, who produce a majority, and often a dissenting, opinion, but in some instances a case is heard *en banc*, by all of the judges serving on the bench for that circuit. A similar model of majority and dissenting opinions is followed on a grander scale with the nine justices of the Supreme Court of the United States. After a summary of the facts and legal procedure as well as the pertinent statutory and common law, a judge's decision and their reasoning are typically organized according to each legal question raised in a case. Within this institutional frame, judges can and do imbue opinions with their own authorial voice and sensibilities.[2] Evocative aphorisms, metaphors, humor, quotations, and even aesthetic value statements exhibit judicial thought processes beyond their interpretation and application of relevant law. Often discounted as *orbiter dictum*, or nonbinding observations that ostensibly do not alter the outcome of a case (sometimes called "dicta"), discerning legal readers are more likely to find temporary amusement in these turns of phrase than critical holdings, or dispositions, of law.[3] Dicta usually appear as either asides from the judge's rationale for the court's decision or as an overly broad claim that cannot be treated as essential to its reasoning.[4] This structure is intended to promote equity and efficiency, both for the court producing the opinion and for readers.

THE "DANGEROUS UNDERTAKING" OF JUDICIAL CRITICISM IN COPYRIGHT LAW

Federal copyright law derives from Article I, Section 8 of the US Constitution, which grants Congress power to create laws that "promote the Progress of Science and the useful Arts by securing for limited Times to Authors and Inventors the exclusive Right to their respective Writings and Discoveries."[5] With the goal of promoting social progress, this broad constitutional language has permitted codification of longstanding public policies that balance the economic interests of creators to be compensated for their work through an exclusive right on the one hand, and broad public access to those works on the other. As applied to US copyright laws, these interests are balanced by enforcement of time limitations on exclusive rights and the maintenance of a communally accessible public domain.[6] Copyright laws are considered "media neutral," in that they are applied similarly across media of expression, from books, maps, and film to music. Many copyright infringement lawsuits therefore consider matters of creative process surrounding fundamental questions of originality and similarity: whether elements shared between copyrighted works are protected by an exclusive right that has been allegedly infringed or whether they are instead a result of independent creation that amounts to unprotectable commonality. For nearly two centuries, judges have sought to define essential terms, to refine methods for assessing similarity, and to identify potential problems, all with the goal of ensuring equitable outcomes across parties and cases.

The 1903 lawsuit of *Bleistein v. Donaldson Lithographing Company* was a landmark for regulating judicial assessments of copyrightable works. In this case, Plaintiff George Bleistein had partnered with the Courier Lithographing Company to design and manufacture three colored posters, or chromolithographs, for "The Great Wallace Shows" traveling circus (Figure 6.1). In April 1898, Courier registered the poster designs with the US Copyright Office and shipped 1,760 pounds of printed posters from their plant in Buffalo, New York, to promoter Benjamin Wallace

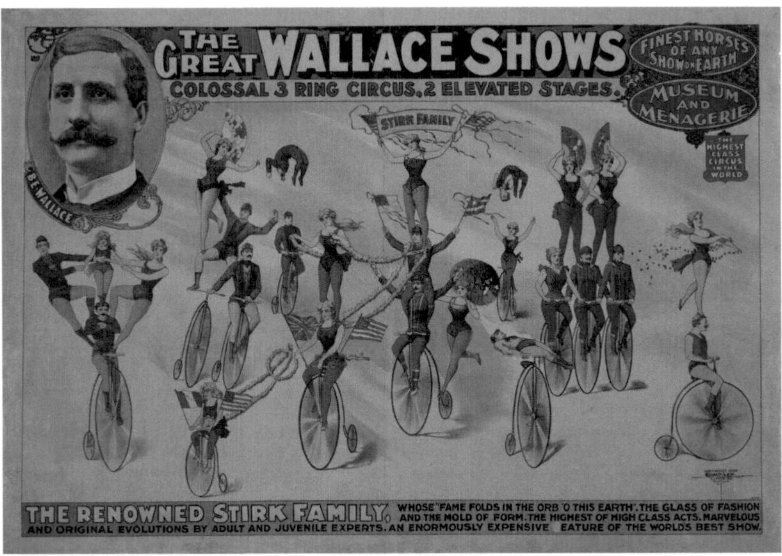

Figure 6.1. Poster for "The Great Wallace Shows"[67]

in Peru, Indiana.[7] Running short on posters, Wallace later hired the Donaldson Lithographing Company, of Newport, Kentucky, to make copies of the same posters. In June 1899, Courier sued Donaldson for infringement. Donaldson leaders were aware of the potential for infringement liability at the time they copied the posters, but they claimed that the posters were merely advertisements and thus unworthy of copyright.[8] The trial court and the Sixth Circuit Court of Appeals accepted Donaldson's defense, because "any engraving, cut, print... or chromo[lithograph]... [must be] connected with the fine arts,"[9] in order to be eligible for copyright protection. Courier, at this point led by Bleistein, appealed.

The Supreme Court reversed the decision on February 2, 1903 by finding in favor of Bleistein, and it remanded—or returned to the district court—the case for a new trial.[10] Writing on behalf of the majority of judges, Justice Oliver Wendell Holmes expressed "profound skepticism" surrounding the ability of judges to assess the quality of copyrighted works.[11] Applying his avocational artistic training to inform his legal reasoning, Justice Holmes explained that the aesthetic value of a work is irrelevant to copyright law:[12]

> It would be *a dangerous undertaking* for persons trained only to the law to constitute themselves final judges of the worth of pictorial illustrations, outside of the narrowest and most obvious limits. At the one extreme, some works of genius would be sure to miss appreciation. Their very novelty would make them repulsive until the public had learned the new language in which their author spoke. [...] At the other end, copyright would be denied to pictures which appealed to a public less educated than the judge. Yet if they command the interest of any public, they have a commercial value—it would be bold to say that they have not an aesthetic and educational value—and the taste of any public is not to be treated with contempt.

Because art can challenge existing aesthetic preferences and understandings, Justice Holmes determined that it was not the role of a judge to determine whether a work was "worthy" of copyright protection. Such subjectivities did not align with the impartial role of judges in resolving disputes, and even if such decisions seemed unavoidable, they should not be imposed on society as tantamount to censorship.[13]

Dissenting Justice John Marshall Harlan disagreed, finding that only works deemed "useful," in accordance with the Constitution, should be considered copyright protectable. The sixth circuit had previously reasoned that copyrightable works were useful only if they have intrinsic value outside of their commercial function, therefore being "connected with the fine arts."[14] Because the posters functioned primarily as advertisements, according to Justice Harlan, they had no additional intrinsic value and should not be copyright protectible.

The *Bleistein* majority decision, which remains binding law at the time of this publication, has been interpreted to shape the low legal threshold required for a copyrightable work to have protectible originality.[15] The Supreme Court majority in this case established an "aesthetic neutrality" principle for copyright law that ostensibly limits judges from allowing such valuations of the works at issue in a case to influence their decisions.[16] In so doing, the 1903 Justices created legal distance between originality as a protectible creative pursuit and notions of progress, usefulness, or artistic merit that might limit the works eligible for copyright protection.

Although no jurisdiction has since adopted an identifiable aesthetic perspective, legal scholarship has demonstrated that aesthetic judgments in a copyright lawsuit may be unavoidable.[17] Scholars have challenged the distinction generated by *Bleistein* between legal and aesthetic reasoning as "illusory," because assessments of originality and similarity necessarily entail aesthetic evaluation, even where additional common law decision-making procedures are applied.[18] "In short, judges necessarily show a preference for certain aesthetic perspectives when they decide cases because copyright law simply requires aesthetic choices."[19] While at least some judges are sensitive to this limitation, over a century of judicial opinions have nevertheless featured dicta that comments on the quality of the works, including music, at issue in each case.

Classifying judges' critical, aesthetic evaluations and their purpose in resolving legal disputes extends the traditional boundaries of musical critique.[20] Like other forms of music criticism, notably journalistic review, judicial opinions depend on individual experience, both of music in the judge's lived past and their perceptions of the parties, as well as the musical works evaluated in each case as objects of critique. Judicial opinions have no predetermined expiration unless they are superseded or overturned, yet as writings about music, they endure as products of their historical and cultural contexts. For these reasons, judicial opinions constitute a previously understudied form of criticism.

MUSICAL CRITIQUE IN THE EARLY TWENTIETH CENTURY

Despite admonition from the *Bleistein* court, judges can, and do, incorporate their own value assessments of the musical works in each case and entire genres in which those works might be classified. This issue appears deeply embedded in the history of music copyright infringement litigation both before and after the US Supreme Court resolved the *Bleistein* case. In the years that immediately followed, early twentieth-century trial judges appear to reify disparities in cultural value between so-called classical music and commercial popular music by devaluing the latter as fleeting, unoriginal, consumable, and at worst, unmusical. These statements represent both individual judicial taste while seeming to align with contemporaneous, communal sentiments of their time toward commercial popular music and ideologies associated with it.[21] They most often appear where judges attempt to locate the limits of copyright protection, notably copyrightable originality, or to create exceptions to otherwise clear rules.[22]

Lawsuits involving early jazz reveal disdain for the new syncopated style. When the Original Dixieland Jazz Band's (ODJB) first commercial jazz record reached music markets in 1917, a lawsuit over authorship of the B-side song, "Livery Stable Blues," soon followed.[23] In *Hart v. Graham*, members of the ODJB and their manager, Max Hart, sued sheet music publisher, Roger Graham, for copyright infringement over the highly similar song he published, titled "Barnyard Blues." In his defense, Graham claimed that both songs were based on archetypal formulas, and therefore unoriginal. Presiding Judge George A. Carpenter, famous for his anti-trust opinions, reportedly ran to his chamber for ice water during the trial testimony from several blues and jazz musicians.[24] Newspaper descriptions of Judge Carpenter's actions might have been exaggerated, but they at least imply social shock over jazz being discussed in the courtroom, a public space believed to be structured by formality and decorum. These reports suggest Judge Carpenter's contempt for jazz aligned with his individual preferences; however, they also seem to reflect contemporaneous public taste that denigrated the emerging style and its creators.[25]

Judge Carpenter's attitude toward early blues and jazz as well as modern avant-garde compositions, are explicitly stated in his case opinion: "no living human being could listen to that result on the phonograph and discover anything musical in it [...] from a musical stand-point it is even out-classed by our modern French dissonance."[26] This section includes no citation to case records or external legal authorities. Based on defense witness testimony that claimed "all blues is alike"[27] and therefore unoriginal, Judge Carpenter dismissed the case—meaning neither the ODJB nor Roger Graham prevailed.

Judge Carpenter's condescension toward both commercial popular genres as well as avant-garde art music showed flagrant disregard for the *Bleistein* decision. His decision to dismiss the case on grounds of a lack of originality in blues, and by extension early jazz, reveals a narrow conception of musical creative process biased against archetypal forms by ignoring sequential revision and contribution as protectible creative acts. The opinion was especially damaging to early blues and jazz as a site of Black musical production, which Judge Carpenter identified in *Hart v. Graham* as a "negro origin"[28] to "Livery Stable Blues."

Although some courts expressed sentimental appreciation for particular composers or songs, judges often cast Tin Pan Alley popular songs as repetitive, unoriginal, or consumable, and therefore of low aesthetic value, in contrast to classical music. The case of *Berlin v. Daigle* is illustrative. In 1926, Irving Berlin sued two sets of business owners over unauthorized public performance of his music: A. Daigle, the owner of a dance pavilion, and brothers Charles and Joseph Russo, co-owners of Russo's Picture Show and Dance Hall. Berlin claimed that the band Daigle hired to perform played three of Berlin's compositions without permission at an event where admission was taken, such that profit could be made in relation to the songs; and, in a similar claim, that the Russo brothers played recordings of the same songs without permission again at an event where admission was collected.[29]

The decisions in these cases are revealing as the court's aesthetic valuation of jazz. Although the claim regarding public performance of the recordings at Russo's establishment was dismissed, the live band case involving Daigle's dance pavilion reached the courtroom. The district court in the Eastern District of Louisiana found that the dance pavilion had infringed on Berlin's copyrights via unlicensed use. Presiding Judge Walker's reasoning revealed his aesthetic stance toward commercial popular music. His decision hinged on explicit critique that "musical compositions such as these popular songs, set to 'jazz' or syncopated tunes" were not "true" orchestral compositions, but "rather only the common garden variety of musical compositions, by the infringement of which no obvious substantial damage is wrought."[30] Although the Fifth Circuit Court of Appeals would later reverse and remand the case for reasons outside of a disregard for *Bleistein*, the case outcome was undoubtedly impacted by the devaluation of Berlin's compositions as "common garden variety," which implied a lack of copyrightable originality.

CONDESCENSION TOWARD COMMERCIAL POPULAR MUSIC: JUDGE LEARNED HAND

Opinions crafted by the inimitable district and appellate Judge Learned Hand are especially critical of commercial popular music. "Music meant a great deal" to Judge Hand, who was an avocational performer and fan of Gilbert and Sullivan operetta.[31] Over his long career serving as a district and appellate court judge, he became known for detailed comparisons of sheet music and often equally detailed commentary in his opinions.[32]

These opinions were explicitly colored by a disdain for commercial popular music and its creators, however, because the judge instead revered Western art music.[33]

Judge Hand's perspective is apparent in the 1910 case of *Hein v. Harris*. Composer Silvio Hein and Marie Cahill, assignee for the rights of lyricist Daniel Arthur, had sued publisher Charles K. Harris. They claimed that Harris's song, "I Think I Hear a Woodpecker Knocking at My Family Tree," which was featured in the musical, *The Golden Girl*, infringed on Hein and Arthur's "The Arab Love Song," from a contemporaneous operetta, *The Boys and Betty*. Judge Hand's opinion included aesthetic valuation of the music, however insulated by reference to witness testimony in support of the defendants:[34]

> the defendant urges *with much truth* that both his own and the complainant's songs are in the *lowest grades* of the musical art. [...] they each bear a strong resemblance to each other, [...] a monotonous similarity, *which only adds to the general degradation of the style of music* which they represent.

In keeping with *Bleistein*, however, Judge Hand wrote later in the opinion that "the lack of originality and musical merit in both songs [...] is of no consequence in law."[35] Judge Hand proceeded to base his decision in favor of plaintiffs Hein and Cahill instead on his own comparative analysis of the published sheet music.[36] This aesthetic valuation would prove to have a detrimental impact on Hein's professional music career, so much so that his attorney wrote to Judge Hand decades later to complain and ask for clarifying commentary or even a reversal of the decision.[37]

Judge Hand's decisions in later cases involving plaintiff-composer Ira Arnstein contain similar attitudes.[38] Arnstein's fifth and final case, this time against famous Tin Pan Alley composer Cole Porter, provoked judges to incorporate aesthetic turns of phrase and—perhaps more importantly for legal specialists—to raise concerns about the relevance of expert musical analysis. The second circuit reversed and remanded the case on grounds that the district court judge's decision-making process was flawed. In their landmark ruling, the majority judges—writing Judge Frank and Judge

Hand—described a legal "test" for evaluating similarity that involved assessments from both nonexpert, or lay, listeners and expert witnesses:[39]

> The plaintiff may call witnesses whose testimony may aid the jury in reaching its conclusion as to the responses of such audiences. Expert testimony of musicians may also be received, but it will in no way be controlling on the issue of illicit copying, and should be utilized only to assist in determining the reactions of lay auditors. The impression made on the refined ears of musical experts or their views as to the musical excellence of plaintiff's or defendant's works are utterly immaterial on the issue of misappropriation; *for the views of such persons are caviar to the general—and plaintiff's and defendant's compositions are not caviar.*

The peculiar, seemingly redundant structure of this decision-making process represented judicial suspicion toward the sophistication of expert witness analyses, considered "caviar to the general."[40] Undoubtedly influenced by Judge Hand, writing Judge Frank extended the culinary metaphor to devalue the perceptions of nonexperts and the music at issue as commonplace by contrasting it to the rare luxury of caviar. The conclusion of this passage transmits a devaluation of popular song: "plaintiff's and defendant's compositions are not caviar."[41]

This instance of dicta might be easily overlooked because it does not justify Judges Frank and Hand's decision to remand the case to the district court with the new test, nor does it directly comment on the risks of aesthetic valuation embedded in the new decision-making process; but it does reveal the second circuit judges' critique of commercial popular song and their suspicion surrounding the discipline-specific detail of musical expert analysis.[42] In the end, the case was unsurprisingly decided in favor of Porter, but it is the idiosyncratic test that the second circuit judges established that has become a foundation for copyright infringement cases even into the present day.[43]

Not every music copyright case contains explicit statements of aesthetic value, and not all federal judges have been as outspoken about commercial popular music as Judge Hand. Other judges appear, at most, dismissive of the value of the lawsuit simply because it involved music "of temporary vogue."[44] These historic cases together comprise an understudied source for contemporaneous social opinions about a lack of value in commercial popular music and the problematic implications of these evaluations with regard to the racial identity of its creators and the scope of legal protection for music. These cases further demonstrate a pattern of judicial disregard for the *Bleistein* case requirement of aesthetic neutrality with implications for the quality of a judge's legal reasoning.

DANGEROUS UNDERTAKINGS: SAMPLING AND CRIMINALITY

While explicit statements devaluing commercial popular music had dwindled from judicial practice by the end of the twentieth century, more recent cases demonstrate an ongoing influence of judicial aesthetic critique. Landmark cases involving sampling feature implicit devaluation through moralizing commentary and even "outright hostility" toward hip-hop creators.[45] Similar to jazz earlier in the century, and correlating with ongoing marginalization of Black music production, judges that confronted hip-hop as a new, and at times socially resistant, musical style seemed to conflate legal reasoning with criticism.[46] As products of their historical and cultural context, these case opinions appear to align with "broader social currents of racial subordination"[47] in the US judicial system, with opinions often featuring extreme outcomes prejudicial to sampling as a creative practice.[48]

Although not the first of its kind, the landmark case of *Grand Upright Music, Ltd. v. Warner Brothers Records, Inc.* set a hostile precedent toward sampling.[49] In this case, Marcel Theo Hall (professionally known as Biz Markie) sampled from "Alone Again," by Irish singer-songwriter Raymond Edward O'Sullivan (professionally known as Gilbert O'Sullivan), in the rap track, "Alone Again (Naturally)." Biz Markie and Warner Brothers sought to negotiate a license to use a sample from the beginning of O'Sullivan's song, but the request was denied. The sample was included despite failed negotiations, so O'Sullivan and Grand Upright soon sued for infringement.[50] In his now infamous opinion, presiding Judge Kevin Duffy opened with a biblical invocation: "Thou shalt not steal."[51] The opinion extended its rhetoric beyond legal reasoning into critical appeals to religious morality:[52]

> the defendants in this action for copyright infringement would have this court believe that stealing is rampant in the music business and, for that reason, their conduct here should be excused. The conduct of the defendants herein, however, violates not only the Seventh Commandment, but also the copyright laws of this country.

Judge Duffy's opinion did not explicitly comment on the aesthetic value of hip-hop or sampling. The written voice and vocabulary of the sensational opening sentences, however, cast sampling as theft, correlating the creative practice with criminality aligned with contemporaneous, racially motivated fears surrounding hip-hop culture.[53] In so doing, the court foregrounded its value judgment about sampling as unoriginal borrowing, rather than a sequential creative process reliant on meaningful quotation, famously classified as "signifyin'."[54] To this end, use of preexisting works becomes a means of representation, transformation, and commentary, and more specifically in the context of sampling in hip-hop, "repetition with a difference."[55] Similar to blues and jazz before it, formal copyright laws fell short of protecting this form of sequential creativity. The case was eventually resolved in O'Sullivan's favor, with Biz Markie required to pay 100 percent royalties of "Alone Again (Naturally)" to O'Sullivan. In a rare and surprising conclusion, Judge Duffy even referred the case for federal criminal prosecution, which was not pursued.[56]

The *Grand Upright* decision set a sanctimonious and aesthetically charged tone for future sampling cases. Commentary surrounding unauthorized sampling appeared again in the 2005 case of *Bridgeport Music, Inc. v. Dimension Films, Inc*, one of several lawsuits separated from the larger case of *Bridgeport Music, Inc. v. 11C Music*.[57] *Bridgeport v. Dimension* involved a two-second guitar sample from the beginning of George Clinton and the Funkadelic's party anthem, "Get Off Your Ass and Jam," which was altered and looped for use in N.W.A.'s 1998 up-tempo rap song, "100 Miles and Runnin'," as heard in the soundtrack to the film, *I Got the Hook-Up*. Although this sample comprised a brief, three-note arpeggiated melodic figure, its repetition, location at the beginning of the Funkadelic song, and whirling prominence in the recorded mix highlighted the originality and importance of the figure to the recognizable identity of "Get Off Your Ass and Jam."[58]

Although the trial court in *Dimension* applied an exception to permit the use of the sample because it was so brief, the sixth circuit famously reversed that decision.[59] The three-judge panel established that sound recording owners had an exclusive right to sample the recordings they controlled; in short, as the court bluntly declared, "Get a license or do not sample."[60] Writing Judge Ralph B. Guy referenced the earlier *Grand Upright* opinion and continued its aesthetic principles by correlating sampling with theft. These critical statements raised the legal stakes for copyright holders and creators alike by pushing sampling toward something more similar to a strict liability scheme, meaning that the identification of a sample would amount to infringement with little, if any, consideration for other creative factors. Relying on an aesthetic interpretation that correlated sampling with theft, the court claimed its ruling would not stifle future musical creativity because:[61]

> When you sample a sound recording you know you are taking another's work product. [...] [E]ven when a small part of a sound recording is sampled, the part taken is something of value. No further proof of that is necessary than the fact that the producer of the record or the artist on the record intentionally sampled because it would (1) save costs, or (2) add something to the new recording, or (3) both.

Although there is no outright aesthetic statement against sampling in the opinion, Judge Guy's misunderstanding of repetition caused by sampling as a creative process generated an unnecessarily strict ruling. At least one scholar has noted that "this passage is naive and ignores many well-publicized examples of sample licenses that are anything but regulated by market demand."[62] Despite ongoing industry opposition and scholarly discourse that reaches an opposite conclusion, the *Dimension* decision has not been overturned and to date has only been outright rejected by one other court.[63]

As products of their time, these and other similar opinions reveal the potential risks of judges critiquing music and the processes of its creative communities, which is often embedded in their legal reasoning and at times even racially prejudicial outcomes. The strict legal conditions surrounding sampling in particular have demonstrably shaped creative practices in hip-hop communities by limiting the scope of protectible originality.[64]

CONCLUSION: RECENT TRENDS AND FUTURE DIALOGUES

Twenty-first-century trends in judicial writing, including the plain-language movement designed to clarify the legibility of legal records, have contributed to shifts in the style of judicial opinions. Although it is possible that recent judges are more attuned to Justice Holmes's 1903 warning in *Bleistein*, word choice can still reveal their critiques. In the 2022 case of *Gray v. Hudson*, for example, contemporary Christian rap artist Marcus Gray (professionally known as "Flame") sued pop artist Katherine Hudson (professionally known as "Katy Perry"), alleging that his song, "Joyful Noise" was infringed on by Perry's electropop hit, "Dark Horse." The musical passage at issue in the case consisted of a repeated descending melody and rhythmic pattern, which prompted discussion of originality. Citing two previous cases from 1940 and 2020, respectively, writing appellate Judge Milan Smith classified this passage as "trite,"[65] and therefore lacking originality. The word choice here is illustrative of perceptions of overuse and unimportance that a less value-laden term, such as "common," could have avoided. Because judges rely on precise, and often precedential, word choice, such deeply embedded aesthetic language is likely to continue to be used in future cases.

Across the history of US federal music copyright, judicial opinions have included aesthetic valuations of protectible works. The 1903 case of

Bleistein v. Donaldson Lithographing Company characterized these assessments as "a dangerous undertaking," prohibiting them for fear of setting unfavorable precedents. Because legal scholars commonly dismiss statements about musical quality as nonbinding, relatively little scholarship has considered the frequency of their occurrence and the extent to which they might shape case outcomes. Framing judicial opinions as criticism begins to expose the historical and cultural rootedness of judicial opinions and the potential of judges' aesthetic valuation to impact their reasoning and, in some instances, even the future of musical creativity. For these reasons, further analysis of judicial aesthetics have much to contribute to discussions of the legal, socioeconomic, and racial dimensions of music copyright.

While future judges would do well to heed Justice Holmes's 1903 warning, only continued cross-disciplinary discourse can generate a "best practices" approach to mitigating the impact of unavoidable judicial aesthetics. In addition to legal scholarship, the growing field of forensic musicology, primarily engaged by music consultants and expert witnesses, is well positioned to assist judges and attorneys. Their academic research and applied forensic reports can offer more nuanced explanations of the nature of music as intellectual property, its diversity of creators, and their creative processes.[66] In the meantime, judicial opinions in federal music copyright litigation continue to merit further study as a "dangerous undertaking" of music criticism.

SAMPLE QUESTIONS FOR DISCUSSION AND FURTHER RESEARCH

1. How might judicial opinions compare to other forms of music criticism? Why might the role of federal judges be different from other music critics?
2. If aesthetic valuations are unavoidable, what steps might legal specialists, either judges or attorneys, take to minimize the impact of such criticism on case outcomes?
3. What resources might musical experts produce to better assist courts in recognizing and accommodating aesthetic judgments?

4. How might current and future copyright laws impact musical creativity?
5. In what ways have judges represented music in the most recent music copyright cases? Do they seem to follow or disregard the *Bleistein* majority?

NOTES

1. For more information on the US legal system, see, e.g., Toni Jaeger-Fine, *The U.S. Legal System: The Basics* (Carolina Academic Press, 2021).
2. William D. Popkin, *Evolution of the Judicial Opinion: Institutional and Individual Styles* (New York University Press, 2007), 2–3, 142–151.
3. See, e.g., Jaeger-Fine, *U.S. Legal System*, 80.
4. See Michael C. Dorf, "Dicta and Article III," *University of Pennsylvania Law Review* 142 (1994): 2007.
5. See US Constitution, Article I, Section 8, Clause 8.
6. See, e.g., David J, Moser and Cheryl L. Slay, *Music Copyright Law* (Cengage Learning, 2012), 3–9.
7. *Courier Lithographing Co. v. Donaldson Lithographic Co.*, 104 F. 993 (6th Cir. 1900), https://case-law.vlex.com/vid/courier-lithographing-co-v-891146283. See also Diane Leenheer Zimmerman, "The Story of Bleistein v. Donaldson Lithographing Company: Originality as a Vehicle for Copyright Inclusivity," in *Intellectual Property Stories*, eds. Jane C. Ginsburg and Rochelle Cooper Dreyfuss (Thomson West, 2006), 78.
8. Zimmerman, "Bleistein v. Donaldson Lithographing," 83–84.
9. *Bleistein v. Donaldson Lithographing Co.*, 188 U.S. 239, 249 (1903), https://supreme.justia.com/cases/federal/us/188/239/.
10. The new trial solely addressed copyright ownership and contract interpretation, and the case eventually settled out of court. See Zimmerman, "Bleistein v. Donaldson Lithographing," 99.
11. Zimmerman, "Bleistein v. Donaldson Lithographing," 78. Zimmerman notes that Justice Holmes found writing this opinion to be "both easy and fun." See Zimmerman, "Bleistein v. Donaldson Lithographing," 95.
12. *Bleistein*, 188 U.S. at 251 (emphasis added).
13. See also Alfred C. Yen, "Copyright Opinions and Aesthetic Theory," *Southern California Law Review* 71 (1998): 248.

14. *Bleistein v. Donaldson Lithographing Co.*, 188 U.S. 239, 251 (1903) (J. Harlan, dissenting) (quoting *Courier Lithographing Co.*, 104 F. at 996).
15. See also *Feist Publications, Inc. v. Rural Telephone Service Co.*, 499 U.S. 340 (1991), https://supreme.justia.com/cases/federal/us/499/340/]; *Burrow-Giles Lithographic Co. v. Sarony*, 111 U.S. 53 (1884), https://supreme.justia.com/cases/federal/us/111/53/.
16. Keith Aoki, "Contradiction and Context in American Copyright Law," *Cardozo Arts & Entertainment Law Journal* 9, no. 2 (1991): 303–38.
17. See generally Robert Kirk Walter and Ben Depoorter, "Unavoidable Aesthetic Judgments in Copyright Law: A Community of Practice Standard," *Northwestern University Law Review* 109, no. 2 (2015): 343–382. See also Yen, "Copyright Opinions and Aesthetic Theory," 249.
18. Yen, "Copyright Opinions and Aesthetic Theory," 251–252.
19. Yen, "Copyright Opinions and Aesthetic Theory," 250 (citation omitted).
20. See, for example, Christopher Dingle, "Introduction," in *The Cambridge History of Music Criticism*, Christopher Dingle, ed. (Cambridge University Press, 2019), 2–3; Fred Everett Maus, Glenn Stanley, Katharine Ellis, Leanne Langley, Nigel Scaife, Marcello Conati et al., "Criticism," Grove Music Online, January 20, 2001, https://doi.org/10.1093/gmo/9781561592630.article.40589.
21. See Mark McKnight, "Music Criticism in the United States and Canada," in *The Cambridge History of Music Criticism*, Christopher Dingle, ed. (Cambridge University Press, 2019): 293–316 (noting that US critics privileged not only Western art music, but specifically mainstream or canonical nineteenth-century compositions over modernist avant-garde works); Fabian Holt, *Genre in Popular Music* (University of Chicago Press, 2007), 2 ("Bourgeois aesthetics valued the notion of the unique and organic art work with a life of its own and that mind-set informed images of popular culture as trivial mass culture derived from mechanical formulae" [citation omitted]).
22. See Popkin, *Evolution of the Judicial Opinion*, 162–167.
23. See Katherine M. Leo, "Early Blues and Jazz Authorship in the Case of the 'Livery Stable Blues,'" *Jazz Perspectives* 12, no. 3 (2020): 311–38, https://doi.org/10.1080/17494060.2020.1833071.
24. See Leo, "Early Blues and Jazz Authorship," 319.
25. See, e.g., Lawrence Levine, "Jazz and American Culture," *The Journal of American Folklore* 102, no. 403 (1989): 6–14, https://doi.org/10.2307/540078.
26. *Hart v. Graham* (N.D. Ill. 1917), Case File E914; U.S. District Court for the Northern District of Illinois, Eastern Division (Chicago), https://blogs.law.gwu.edu/mcir/case/hart-v-graham/.

27. See Leo, "Early Blues and Jazz Authorship," 334.
28. *Hart v. Graham* (N.D. Ill. 1917). See K. J. Greene, "'Copynorms,' Black Cultural Production, and the Debate over African-American Reparations," *Cardozo Arts and Entertainment Journal* 25, no. 3 (2008): 1185–6; Leo, "Early Blues and Jazz," 21–22.
29. Berlin, who by that time had become a successful songwriter and entrepreneur, sued for the minimum statutory damages amount available at the time for "orchestral compositions." These two cases are unusual because Berlin's stake does not appear to reflect the same monetary motivation as in other copyright lawsuits. Plaquemine continues to be the parish seat in Iberville, Louisiana, but in 1926, it was not a large metropolitan area. Any economic impact of public performance of Berlin's music would have been limited, and the band musicians likely performed either with this negligent assumption or under the mistaken belief that they could legally use the sheet music as the basis for improvisation. See *Berlin v. Daigle*, 26 F.2d 149, 149 (E.D. La. 1928), *rev'd* 31 F.2d 832 (5th Cir. 1929), https://casetext.com/case/irving-berlin-v-daigle].
30. *Berlin*, 26 F.2d at 150.
31. Gerald Gunther, *Learned Hand: The Man and the Judge* (Oxford University Press, 2011), 271.
32. Gunther, *Learned Hand*, 37, 269–71. Hand has been said to have particularly enjoyed writing music copyright decisions. He produced two recordings for the Archive of American Folk Song at the Library of Congress during a visit to Washington, D.C., in 1942. See Ross E. Davies, "Learned Hand Sings, Part One: Liner Notes for 'Songs of His Youth'," *Green Bag* 16 (2013): 257–80. https://doi.org/10.2139/ssrn.2271070. For the recording, see Judge Learned Hand Recordings (AFC 1945/007), Archive of Folk Culture, American Folklife Center, Library of Congress, Washington, DC; Learned Hand, *Songs of His Youth* (GBRC 2013-1). See also Katherine Leo, "Musical Expertise and the 'Ordinary' Listener in Federal Copyright Law," *Music and Politics* 13, no. 1 (2019): 3 n.10–11. https://doi.org/10.3998/mp.9460447.0013.108.
33. Gunther, *Learned Hand*, 269. See also Katherine Leo, *Forensic Musicology and the Blurred Lines of Federal Copyright History* (Lexington, 2021), 36–40; Leo, "Musical Expertise," 2–4.
34. *Hein v. Harris*, 175 F.875, 876 (S.D.N.Y. 1910) (emphasis added), https://caselaw.vlex.com/vid/hein-v-harris-894476563.
35. *Hein*, 175 F. at 877.
36. *Hein v. Harris*, 175 F.875, 876 (S.D.N.Y. 1910), *aff'd* 183 Fed. 107 (2d Cir. 1923), https://blogs.law.gwu.edu/mcir/case/hein-v-harris/.

37. Hand deflected blame onto a misrepresentation made by the appellate court bench. He wrote that the Second Circuit was "clear off in saying that for copyright infringement it was necessary that the defendant should borrow from the plaintiff. They mixed up the rule between patents and copyrights and have since that time repudiated it, so the law is on a sound basis now." The opinion in that case, however, was an affirmance of Hand's own district court opinion. Gunther, *Learned Hand*, 634–35 n.114.
38. See, e.g., *Arnstein v. Edward B. Marks Music Corp.*, 82 F.2d 275, 277 (2d Cir. 1936) [hereinafter *Marks*], https://law.justia.com/cases/federal/appellate-courts/F2/82/275/1500419/. For more on Arnstein, see generally Gary A. Rosen, *Unfair to Genius: The Strange and Litigious Career of Ira B. Arnstein* (Oxford University Press, 2012).
39. *Arnstein v. Porter*, 154 F.2d 465, 473 (2d Cir. 1946) (emphasis added), https://blogs.law.gwu.edu/mcir/case/arnstein-v-porter/. For a detailed discussion of the case, see Leo, *Forensic Musicology*, 59–69.
40. For an earlier instance of disdain toward nonexpert analyses, see, e.g., *Haas v. Leo Feist, Inc.*, 234 F. 105 (S.D.N.Y. 1916) ("it is perfectly apparent to unsophisticated common-sense"), https://blogs.law.gwu.edu/mcir/case/haas-v-leo-feist/.
41. *Arnstein*, 154 F.2d at 473.
42. See Yen, "Copyright Opinions and Aesthetic Theory."
43. See, e.g., Leo, *Forensic Musicology*, 82–83.
44. *Boosey v. Empire Music*, 224 F. 646 (S.D.N.Y. 1915), https://blogs.law.gwu.edu/mcir/case/booseyempire/. See, e.g., *Fred Fisher, Inc. v. Dillingham*, 298 F. 145 (S.D.N.Y. 1925) ("the controversy is a 'trivial pother'"), https://blogs.law.gwu.edu/mcir/case/fred-fisher-inc-v-dillingham/.
45. Greene, "'Copynorms,'" 1185–6.
46. See, e.g., Christopher Deis, "Hip-Hop and Politics," in *The Cambridge Companion to Hip-Hop*, Justin A. Williams, ed. (Cambridge University Press, 2015), 192.
47. Greene, "Copynorms," 1186.
48. See, e.g., Charles Cronin, "Race in the Courthouse: Less Protection as More Equal Protection for Musical Works," *Hastings Communications and Entertainment Law Journal* 43, no. 2 (Summer 2021): 175.
49. See Amanda Sewell, "How Copyright Affected the Musical Style and Critical Reception of Sample-Based Hip-hop," *Journal of Popular Music Studies* 26, no. 2–3 (2014): 295 (noting earlier sampling settlements involving the Beastie Boys), http://dx.doi.org/10.17613/M6JG2P; Greene, "'Copynorms,'" 1186.
50. See also Leo, *Forensic Musicology*, 118–120.

51. *Grand Upright Music, Ltd. v. Warner Bros. Records, Inc.*, 780 F. Supp. 182, 183 (S.D.N.Y. 1991), https://blogs.law.gwu.edu/mcir/case/grand-upright-v-warner/.
52. *Grand Upright*, 780 F. Supp. at 183.
53. Deis, "Hip-hop and Politics," 200–201.
54. See Justin A. Williams, *Rhymin' and Stealin': Musical Borrowing in Hip-Hop* (University of Michigan, 2013), 3; Samuel A. Floyd Jr., *The Power of Black Music: Interpreting Its History from Africa to the United States* (Oxford University Press, 1995), 7–8, 95–96.
55. Williams, *Rhymin' and Stealin'*, 3 (quoting Russell Porter).
56. *Grand Upright*, 780 F. Supp. at 185.
57. *Bridgeport v. 11C Music*, 202 F.R.D. 229 (M.D. Tenn. 2001), https://casetext.com/case/bridgeport-music-inc-v-11c-music-2003].
58. *Bridgeport Music, Inc. v. Dimension Films*, Stewart Declaration, 5–7. See also Leo, *Forensic Musicology*, 126–128.
59. The legal maxim *de minimis non curat lex*, or "the law does not concern itself with trifles," meaning seemingly small, inconsequential matters. See *West Pub. Co. v. Edward Thompson Co.*, 169 F. 833, 861 (E.D.N.Y. 1909) ("Even where there is some copying, that fact is not conclusive of infringement. Some copying is permitted"), https://case-law.vlex.com/vid/west-pub-co-v-895358961.
60. *Bridgeport Music, Inc. v. Dimension Films*, 410 F.3d 792, 801 (6th Cir. 2005), https://blogs.law.gwu.edu/mcir/case/bridgeport-music-v-dimension-films-et-al/.
61. *Bridgeport v. Dimension*, 410 F.3d at 801–02.
62. Joanna Demers, "Sound-Alikes, Law, and Style," *University of Missouri Kansas City Law Review* 83, no. 2 (2014): 308.
63. See *VMG Salsoul v. Ciccone*, 824 F.3d 871 (9th Cir. 2016), https://blogs.law.gwu.edu/mcir/case/vmg-salsoul-llc-v-madonna-louise-ciccone-et-al/.
64. Sewell, "How Copyright Affected Sample-Based Hip-Hop," 319; Williams, *Rhymin' and Stealin'*, 2.
65. *Gray v. Hudson*, 28 F.4th 87, 97-98 (9th Cir. 2022), https://blogs.law.gwu.edu/mcir/case/marcus-gray-et-al-v-katy-perry-et-al/.
66. Leo, "Forensic Musicology."
67. Poster advertisement, "The Great Wallace Shows," Library of Congress Prints and Photographs Division (1898), accessed August 15, 2024, https://www.loc.gov/resource/cph.3g13545/.

CHAPTER SEVEN

"SHOULD I PERFORM THIS MUSIC?"

Tony Perman, Deborah Wong, Putu Hiranmayena, Nkululeko Zungu, and Renata Yazzie[I]

We, the authors, contain multitudes. We share a passion for music, the conviction that it is meaningful, and a commitment to music education. But our respective passions, convictions, and commitments emerge from diverse identities, positionalities, and experiences in relation to the structures of power and inequality in which we live and play. This has led each of us to different disciplinary and institutional homes, areas of expertise, and approaches to making and understanding music. But we all write in English (although not exclusively), reside in the United States (at least some of the time), and care deeply about what undergraduate students think. Questions of appropriation matter to us as musicians and educators and we hope our collective reflections offer you something worthwhile as you navigate your own musical ethics. Hopefully, one of our voices will speak to you.

THE ORIGINS OF THE CHART

Tony Perman
Professor of Music, Grinnell College

My students worry about **cultural appropriation.**[2] Those who self-identify as occupying positions of privilege are often afraid that they'll impose their values on marginalized others, thus finding various reasons *not* to engage with difference. Others are defensive about the discussion regarding cultural appropriation and fear their artistic **freedom** will be constrained. Still others, who feel they have been subjected to systemic bias are exhausted from being imposed upon by others, and often look to enforce boundaries of distinction and exclusion. These anxieties around appropriation inhibit students' behavior and will to learn despite their sincere desire to engage with the world around them, to understand **communities** other than their own, and to potentially use music to do it. I've immersed myself in these questions partly because teaching students about the value of diversity and cross-cultural interaction is an essential element of a liberal education, but also, quite simply, because I want students to study the Zimbabwean mbira with me and learn about musical life in deeply embodied ways.[3] I think it can improve their lives. Engaging with difference through music and dance is vital to our humanity and a powerful tool in overcoming the seemingly intractable structural inequities of the day. Of course, the fact that these engagements can also be complicit in acts of cultural erasure or misunderstanding makes it all the more important to consider them thoughtfully and carefully. The potential risks and rewards of musical boundary-crossing both make thoughtful reflection an essential exercise.

However, it is increasingly complicated for me, as a white American performer of a Zimbabwean instrument, to navigate the ethical morass that accompanies our shared musicking. It is difficult to provide clarity when a student asks, "Should I **perform** this music?" when there are so many variables to consider. Even if many musical interactions fall short of "theft," there are still complex potential ethical consequences. When my student responded to the possibility of learning an endangered language by saying "That's not my language to speak," I felt compelled to confront the equation balancing artistic and epistemic freedom, cross-cultural communication, **mutual obligation**, **empathy**, and an **acknowledgment** of the intractable legacies of colonialism, racism, and patriarchy. On the one hand, I want to embolden students to overcome their fear, create, and explore the world. On the other hand, I want them to learn how to recognize and accept the potential consequences of those explorations and to consider how their actions either reinforce or undermine structural norms. Danielle Brown shook ethnomusicology and music education to their core with her open letter calling out these disciplines for their complicity in perpetuating colonial inequalities and anti-Black racism.[4] Simultaneously, Indigenous scholars across the world challenged ethnomusicology and related disciplines to do better in correcting the legacies of settler colonialism.[5] While there have been many calls to "**decolonize**" disciplines like ethnomusicology by "giving back" epistemological space to Indigenous perspectives, there is also a recognition, thanks to Tuck and Yang, that decolonization itself cannot operate as a metaphor that evades structural change or substantive redress.[6]

I developed the chart below (Figure 7.1) to initiate a conversation with my students during a class called "Performing Difference" in 2021. Students were often confused during our discussions of the complex questions any potential engagement with cultural difference would raise. The logical train of thought would splinter into too many directions to access clarity. I hoped a visual representation of these logical paths would allow each student to navigate these ethical quandaries in their own time. We explored the dynamics of cultural appropriation, the limits of freedom, the value of "world music" **ensembles**, and the musical tools people use to negotiate boundaries of self and other in ways good, bad, and ambiguous. My goal was to communicate the complex dynamics behind questions of cultural appropriation and inspire ethical consideration among my students. Evaluating cultural appropriation and other creative engagements with difference is incredibly complicated. My hope, when crafting this chart, was to urge students along a path of critical self-reflection that relied on simple questions and required them to engage with difficult ethical contingencies. In class, I think it worked best when engaged with a specific instance of performance across boundaries of difference in mind.

Since then, I've thought about the chart many times. Unfortunately, it's always me doing the thinking. Productive or not, this chart is trapped by my own biases, training, and experience. These questions have become so fundamental to music education writ large that I feel compelled to learn from and receive diverse perspectives. To that end, I've shared the chart you see here with several scholars and musicians whom I respect, with very different perspectives, experiences, and training: Deborah Wong, Putu Hiranmayena, Nkululeko Zungu, and Renata Yazzie. I gave each of them the freedom to respond and critique however they saw fit. They didn't see any of the text you see here in advance, so that they could respond without prejudice. We are all music educators, but we collectively represent diverse ages, career stages, musical subdisciplines, places of origin, and identities. This diversity not only makes it more likely that something one of us says will speak to you, but is also presented as an acknowledgment that diverse perspectives from multiple subject positions are essential components of humanistic inquiry. No one musical tradition or community ought to occupy the center of our musical and ethical reflections. Once you have grappled with the chart itself, I invite you to read our reflections in whatever order you choose. Each offers a different perspective with different lessons. Each exposes shortcomings and gaps in the chart that I likely wouldn't have recognized on my own. My own reflection will dig deeper on why I made the chart and what I hope to gain from presenting it to you in this rather unusual format.

Now I offer it to you. I hope you take the chart seriously, but it is also meant to be fun. The questions themselves are meant to make you really consider your values and knowledge. Claiming music as one's own, acknowledging histories of oppression, or predicting what your interpersonal relationships will be in the future don't lend themselves to easy, fixed, or agreed-upon answers, but the goal isn't to "get the right answer," but to take seriously that musical choices carry ethical weight rooted in the dynamics of history. At its heart, I made this chart to provide a tool for asking, along with my students, whether our choices live up to our values. You might find it better, in the long run, to design your own. If you're not a visual learner, you might come up with other mechanisms to tackle these ethical dynamics. The questions posed here may also implicitly prioritize specific subjectivities over others. Since I am the one who made it, they likely prioritize those reminiscent of my own. In other words, if you identify as occupying a position of privilege, this chart will likely speak to you differently than if you occupy a more marginalized position. But as you begin, just know that whatever music you have in mind, it is very important to somebody. It has a history wrapped up in multiple other complex histories. Because nothing is static and your decision to play, to listen, or to share music beyond the borders of your own community is a small contribution to that history. Your actions will impact the dynamics of that music's meaning, however subtly.

The next step is up to you. I share my thought process below, but I leave it to you whether or not to skip ahead or start with the chart. When engaging with difference through sound and performance, there are no easy answers. There are only potential risks and potential rewards. Be bold with the knowledge that creativity can be an act of resistance if you want it to be but can also be an act of complicity if you allow it to be. As you put yourself into the chart below, I urge you to be specific about who you are and what sounds you hope to engage. "Perform" appears in the title, but it could be defined as loosely as suits your life, even if it means playing something quietly at home on your own, wearing a specific item of clothing for the first time as you assert a sense of self, or listening to music you know nothing about. As you encounter the question "Do I claim it as my own?", define the terms "I," "claim," and "own" in whatever way seems authentic to your experience and moves the exercise forward. Every gesture or choice intimated by the chart invites divergence and disagreement—that is the point. I loved *Choose Your Own Adventure* books as a kid and invite you to choose your own here and then let my collaborators and I challenge your thinking as you go.

So, whoever you are, whether an educator, undergraduate, musician, or music scholarship junkie, think of a music you admire and might consider playing (Reggae? Bluegrass? Hip-hop? Opera? Salsa? Jazz? Afrobeats? Gamelan? Baroque chamber music? Gospel?) and ask yourself...

Should I perform this music?

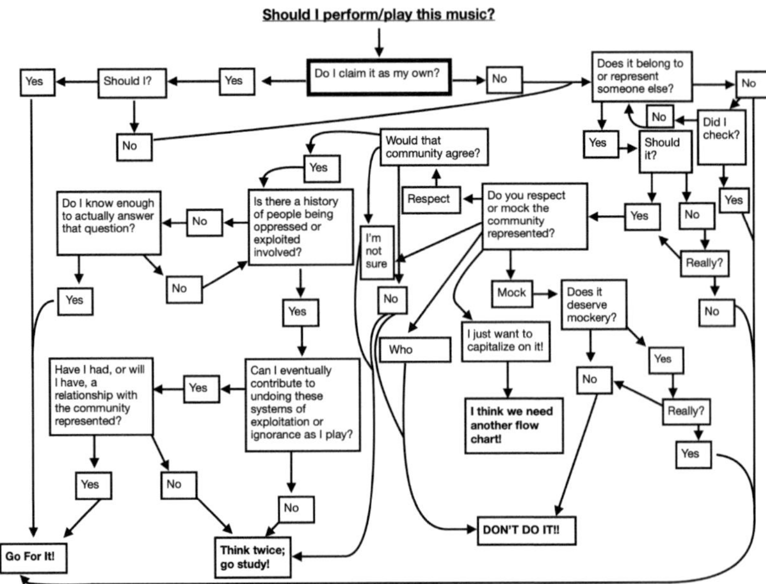

Figure 7.1. The chart, created by Tony Perman

RESPONSE #1

Tony Perman

Why did I make this chart? I'm from rural Illinois, but I've played the mbira from Zimbabwe since meeting Chartwell Dutiro in London, England in 1996.[7] Unlike my collaborators here, I am raced by both myself and others as white. And unlike some of them, I am an ethnomusicologist. The nexus of these two claims leads me to examine my own work as a musician, educator, and scholar in relation to the reality that ethnomusicology, as a discipline, is a product of colonialism. As someone who has played and taught the Zimbabwean mbira for over twenty years, I have thought long and hard about what it means to do so as a white, male, agnostic, US citizen. Sustained attention to my responsibilities toward the students I introduce to the mbira has increasingly consumed much of my professional energy.

As a point of comparison, I often think and teach about the banjo. With roots in West Africa and a period of transformation in the Caribbean, the banjo's shift from being played exclusively by Black performers in the Americas to being played almost exclusively by European Americans as the quintessential expression of whiteness, makes clear the damage that thoughtless appropriation can do.[8] Despite being at the center of so many vibrant and healthy communities now, the banjo was essentially stolen and redefined by white players, through both "love and theft," as Eric Lott puts it.[9] Its original purpose and attachment to community were ignored, erased, and rewritten. That is the risk of cultural appropriation.

The definition of cultural appropriation that I use in my own life as a musician and an educator comes from my colleague Moyo Mutamba. When he spoke to my students from his perspective as a Zimbabwean mbira player, DEI consultant, and social justice advocate, he defined cultural appropriation as "the use of cultural materials or expressions from an oppressed community without relationships to that community." You could argue that I have appropriated his definition, but there is an element of acknowledgment analogous to academic honesty in dynamics of ethical appropriation. I am indebted to Moyo for his insight and center that indebtedness. By citing him and acknowledging his influence on me, I hope that my own act of appropriation is a step in a budding interpersonal relationship. His definition touches on the variables I consider most when tackling these ethical quandaries: use, oppression, community, and relationships.

But these variables don't only emerge when performing. Even listening can cause harm. Dylan Robinson tells the story of listening in solidarity with other Canadian First Nations' audience members to an opera

(*Louis Riel*) with an aria based on a composition (*Kuyas* by Harry Somers) based on a Nisga'a melody (a limx' ooy, "dirge sung for the passing of a family member") collected by the ethnographer Marius Barbeau in 1927.[10] Unfortunately

> To sing a limx' ooy outside of the appropriate ceremonial context and by someone other than the hereditary rights holder is not just to break Nisga'a law, but also to release its spirit, which can have negative impacts on the lives of the singers and the listeners.[11]

He describes his own refusal to hear (with his hands over his ears) and the experience of witnessing his compatriots' grief with an urgent recognition of the need for repair. He says, "For the next hour, they explained to me in detail the violence that they heard, how they witnessed brutality inflicted on a loved one".[12] Most of the audience members around them knew nothing of this story, socialized in the histories of extraction that defined North American settler colonialism. They passively received the aria as a mere melody, to be judged "aesthetically" and nothing more. Should I listen to this music? The answer will vary depending on who you are, where you are, and who else is involved. I don't know anyone from the Nisga'a community, and I'm certainly not a hereditary rights holder, so my descent down the chart leads me to no: "Don't do it!"

But responding to these truths by withdrawing and solidifying boundaries of identity between communities is also risky. The rewards of engaging with others through sound and movement are vast. Initiating relationships through practices of listening and collaboration can be foundational for community-building, activism, anti-racist resistance, and advocacy for oppressed and marginalized communities. That's why the question I began with on the chart, before surrounding it with complexity, was "Can you eventually contribute to undoing systems of exploitation and ignorance as you play?" Regardless of the details of your answer, I would argue that all learning based on what other people value and cherish must take the question seriously if that learning and playing is to be responsibly done.

This chart is, I hope, not a shortcut but a means toward sifting through which complexities and dynamics matter most on the creative path you are following. Performing across variables of difference can feel false at first, like a form of mimicry. But when done sincerely and with an awareness of the accompanying responsibilities and obligations of acknowledgment and debt that accompany it, such creative engagement can change who you are and how you relate to the world; it can make you care for people who you may otherwise rarely consider; it may lead you to advocate on their behalf. In return they may advocate on yours. Communities can be built in such ways across boundaries that histories of racism, white supremacy, and patriarchy have made seem unimpeachable. Kathleen Higgins celebrates music as a path toward peace, social harmony, and other "humanizing ends."[13] While I perhaps see more risk than she does, I ultimately agree that breaking down the barriers that divide people through musical practice can be a beautiful thing. But the ethics of doing so are elusive, contingent, and variable from one instance to the next. For Paisley Rekdal, appropriation "enlarges, rather than shrinks, our sense of connection by requiring us to interrogate the historically enmeshed relationships we have, and don't have, with one another."[14] To approach appropriation with ethical seriousness is to reevaluate the values that you claim to hold, think about how art may have failed us, and acknowledge how it has inspired change.

RESPONSE #2

Deborah Wong
Professor of Ethnomusicology, University of California, Riverside

A piece of music is playing in my head. I've danced it repeatedly since 2013—at least a hundred times. The song implies its dance, so I can't hear it without my body mentally following it. This song contains the hopes of social justice workers who are modeling ways to connect across difference. They ask one another: *How can we connect in ethical, principled, and respectful ways?* They are doing the thing that will result in new music that you or I will then need to ask ourselves: *Should I play this music?* They asked those same questions as preconditions for writing the music to which I now dance. They worked together using a set of guidelines that resulted in ethical (and beautiful, joyous) music.

I hope you spend time traveling through this amazing chart, exploring its marshes, byways, deltas, and headwaters. Its pathways don't give you many hiding places where you can delude yourself by retreating to First World privilege. The chart won't allow you to use other people for your own pleasures. That very first question, that point of entry—*Do I claim it as my own?*—should make you stop and think hard about what *claiming* is, isn't, or shouldn't be. Did you get to *yes* a little too quickly? Did you realize that you shouldn't push past that first question as if it were a simple turnstile?

United States-trained scholars in the humanities are very well trained in critique, and we often go straight to critique. We often assume that assessment is the same as critique, and critique is understood as a thoughtful process of close reading with a focus on both strengths and weaknesses... but especially weaknesses, shortcomings, or vulnerabilities. Critique is thus often wielded sharply or even ruthlessly, and most humanities-based thinkers are very good at it.

In my view, this chart is not primarily a method of critique. Instead, it offers essential critical handles that are meant to redirect and channel musical decision-making. It can't do all the work for us. It offers abundant opportunities for critique, but it never stops there. It jumps off from critical scholarship addressing cultural appropriation but is directed differently. It sets in motion a process quite different from the everyday, commonsensical, unsurprising critique that is everywhere in music scholarship. That kind of critique is important and utterly necessary, but it is rarely directed toward generative models for doing better. This chart shows some ways to do better. Its binary options are deceptive. It's open-ended, and it relies on an agentive, thoughtful musician who enters the process with the willingness to consider *not* playing this music. If you want to justify what you already intend to do, neither this chart nor anyone else will likely stop you. Instead, this chart puts ethical intent squarely in your hands. It's literally meant to be *used*—not 'studied' but *put to use*, because ethical decision-making must be a practice (and not an abstract exercise).

So, who are you and what is your intent? My sense is that the chart was created for educated, probably white musicians who have access to sounds from near and far. I'm a multiethnic Asian American woman who grew up in the political tumult of the 1960s. I spend most of my time—intentionally!—with artists, scholars, and cultural workers focused on social justice work. When I imagine them using this chart, I see them looking closely and eagerly at it, because social justice workers know we can only get to where we want to be by activating good processes. Good processes are more important than specific outcomes and goals. The utopian ideal of a just world may seem like a retreating horizon but it's not out of reach, and in the meantime, we must work together using processes that broadcast and imagine the just futures for which we long. My social-justice-worker colleagues will approach this chart with the intent of learning how to do better, and we can't have too many good models for strong work that is anti-racist, decolonial, and anti-appropriative.

Don't you want to know what song is running through my head? It's "Bam Butsu—no Tsunagari (10,000 Things, All Connected),"[15] co-created by Nobuko Miyamoto, César Castro, Quetzal Flores, and Martha González.[16] This song and its participatory dance are the result of deep personal friendships across ethnicity and contiguous Japanese American and Chican@ neighborhoods in Los Angeles. As Martha Gonzalez writes, this song emerged from joyful and intentional "co-convening," a radical method that she and Quetzal Flores have developed over many years. As she puts it, "the intent to establish cross-cultural traditions of music and dance in the United States is, in its simplest terms, a pushback on the persistent isolation capitalist society inflicts on us all."[17] The song was co-created with principled intent. Whenever anyone steps into the circle to sing or dance it, they are drawn into the spirit and methods of co-convening. Their feet trace a pathway much like Tony Perman's chart. The chart assumes (indirectly) that music is reproduction: *should*

I play this music? mostly (I think) means *should I (re)produce these sounds?*, whereas my artivista colleagues created a song that invites principled co-convening, or making culture through encounter, rather than reproduction.

We can't undo history, but we can explore methods for doing better. This chart is one such method. Use it!

RESPONSE #3

Putu Hiranmayena
Assistant Professor of Music (Creativity), Grinnell College

While musical worlds collide and cultural identity is interrogated, students studying music can feel stifled with the growing social weight of activist fatigue and option paralysis. For students who want to do right by the world as musicians but can't find the right path (or action), how can we as educators help? I frame this piece around ideas that endorse proactive pathways of action for a more informed inquiry concerning right or wrong choices in musical performance.

I begin from the perspective of an international Indonesian artist-scholar who has lived between Indonesia and the United States for over thirty years. I have traversed professional lines of academia, performance, composition, and public sector work, while seeing no separation of cultural arts from quotidian life. Performing identity has never been removed from my pedagogical methods of engaging with traditional and contemporary Balinese arts; at every instance, having to code switch and negotiate representations of identity relative to local and global communities. Ultimately, my positionality is naturally amorphous, contextual, and is a foundation of cultural negotiation from which my response to the flowchart stems.

As a tool for critical inquiry, the "Should I perform this music?" flowchart offers a good introduction into the epistemologies of performing equity. Although its visual component could use design modifications to clarify pathways of action, the ocular-centric noise alludes to the complexities of negotiating questions of musical appropriation and points to how many people tend to confront topics of cultural representation. For a person that is just beginning to think critically about the role of sound and performance ethno-aesthetics, it provides a basic trajectory of how to engage with music that potentially occupies and transcends borders. Thus, instead of focusing on what components or questions might be missing, my response to the flowchart highlights an autoethnographic perspective rooted in endorsements of creative ethnographic methodologies.

The notion of livelihood as it is fed through this web of interaction is one that compels me to think about appropriation in global economies. Many native practitioners of cultural musics—that which are at least conceptually tied to a sense of national or ethnic identity—are situated, at this point, outside of their home countries. There are myriad reasons for migrating out of one's home—religious persecution, political instability, socioeconomic degradation, and so on—but the prospects of creating a livelihood from sharing one's music are unique to the traditions in which they come from. From teaching a gamelan ensemble in a nonprofit organization; to performing Hindustani music at a local restaurant; to hosting Balkan social events; to diasporic Ghanaian spirit events; to many more examples of people and communities creating life in new lands, each must decide how to present themselves as a way to survive and participate relative to and in new localities. One of the aspects of this flowchart that makes for viable importance is the decision and choices to engage with artforms that come with being new residents of a community. I see this as an empathetic way of engaging with difference and necessary for respecting human diversity. An example of this is a growing phenomenon that comes from neoliberal fear that has people disengaging with topics that directly pertain to personal identity politics. This presumes that confrontation with difference should be isolated and unacknowledged, which then promotes a power differential that values ideological gatekeeping and vocal suppression, thus, for example, contributing to global music ensembles getting scrapped from university programs and people having normal day jobs instead of practicing their artistic culture. On the other side of the spectrum is when settler colonialists come into a new country and exploit local arts by teaching it themselves as a way to create a livelihood of overstaying immigration visas and thus taking away opportunities from native musicians. Finicky financial earnings become even more unstable. We see this far too frequently when foreign practitioners capitalize on other musics of people that still exist (often, their teachers) and have no intention to include them in conversation or financial gain.

In moving through the flowchart, the idea of what I'm calling adjacent materiality comes to mind. That is, how new instruments are made that take inspiration from global musical idioms, such as new gamelan made by Lou Harrison; or lamellaphones that are made from recycled material modeled from mbira; or even ukuleles made from cigar boxes. Are these instruments subject to similar critique, or are they tangible spaces to bypass appropriation and ultimately contribute to legacies of human creativity? I will not attempt to answer that here, but it does help to remind us of the importance of communal composition and what occupying the Homi Bhabhaian "third space" can afford: a space Bhabha describes as providing potential for new discourse and cultural negotiation to arise, largely due to intersections of colliding cultures.[18] With the guidance of cultural ambassadors in teaching idioms of musical culture, new communal works can offer people a sense of identity that is nuanced to microlocality. This space of convergence may be why fusion musics are sociocultural utopias and spaces for dialectics of difference.

The flowchart's simplicity allows for the subjectivities of the reader to take precedent and affords a personal agency in contextualizing problems for themselves. A person who is thinking about mascots in sporting events and the musico-physiological responses to game—such as the "tomahawk chop" or stereotypical Native American sonorities—could be thinking about the grotesque representation of Native American identity, but see how a non-Native person who grew up in that community could hear it as a soundtrack of local unity. And although this flowchart is heuristic, it seems interested in expressing and highlighting empathetic morals. Hopefully, people would come out of the flowchart making careful decisions.

Addendum: I offer an example of my own approaches to the importance of communal composition and sustainability of creativity. This past academic year (2022–2023) was my first year teaching as assistant professor of music (performance and creativity) at Grinnell College in Iowa. Under my authority, the music department purchased a set of Balinese gamelan instruments that are relatively unorthodox: a mixture of multiple kinds of idiomatic Balinese gamelan (that is, *selonding*, *baleganjur*, *gambuh*, *samara dana*). I commissioned the gamelan from various makers in Bali and tuned the set to itself for the prospects of mixing and matching styles. Students at Grinnell College could then explore the sonic diversity of Balinese gamelan while learning how to compose pieces that they could call their own. This way, they would be afforded opportunities to honor living traditions and experiment with the dynamics of their own artistic communities: an ideal that is embedded in Balinese traditions. At the end of the year, we hosted a public naming ceremony that included members of the Meskwaki Nation to help bless the ensemble in this public ceremony of interfaith animism. We then marked the moment by Professor Emeritus Roger Vetter and Valerie Vetter (who previously taught Javanese gamelan at Grinnell College) sounding the new gongs. The Balinese Sound Ensemble, Tari Dasar Class, and Gender in Balinese Dance Class then shared their compositions and choreography of neotraditional *kreasi* pieces, which culminated in a spontaneous *kecak* (Balinese chanting) with the audience. We decided on the name, "Gamelan Pawisik" which roughly translates to cosmological whispers and utterances of ethereality. This name characterizes the ensemble based on locality and aura of community. The beautiful rolling hills of Iowa have whispered comfort, contention, and malleability. And in true Balinese linguistic play, the name "Pawisik" also sounds like "Poweshiek," the county Grinnell is in and the name of revered Meskwaki chief. In establishing the Balinese music and dance programs at Grinnell, we have combined and honored the artistic traditions in which I am a part, the charge to experimentation that is built into these traditions, communal exploratory artistic voices, and the specific context and history of the site where we do our work today. I offer this as an anecdote that presents hope by inspiring combination of artistic agency and cultural stewardship that fuses curation and creation.

RESPONSE #4

Nkululeko Zungu
DMA Student in Music Composition, University of Georgia

There is no better time than the present to ponder such a prompt as, "Should I perform this music?" As a student currently completing a doctoral degree in music, I have found that I am often asking myself the same question. Because I identify as African, Black, and queer, it is pertinent that I consciously navigate uncomfortable territories while attempting to answer such a prompt. So I am thoroughly pleased to offer a humble response to Dr. Perman's flow diagram to continue the discourse on such a global research question.

The answer to "Should I perform this music?" is not an easy one, as the diagram displays, and it should not be easy. In many cultures, music is used for various reasons beyond entertainment. In the music practices of the Shona with the mbira *dzavadzimu,* the Mande empire in the *jeliya* practice, or even in the music of Skwatta Kamp in the *kwaito* genre (I am using examples from the African continent, but the same can be said for many cultures in the rest of the world), the music is rooted in traditions that aim to preserve and express many cultures. As outsiders (or even insiders) of a particular type of music, we do not get to diminish history. Thus, anyone new to the music therefore has a responsibility to do their best to honor and respect the art they want to perform; otherwise, one may fall trap to disrespecting a group or multiple groups of people by misrepresenting them sonically. This is why the first and most central questions of the flowchart are "Do I claim it as my own?" and "Does it belong to, or represent someone else?"

There are two areas on the diagram where I believe a restructuring may be beneficial. The first comes after the question, "Did I check?" which follows the question, "Does it belong to, or represent someone else?" According to the flow, if one answers "yes" to this question, one may be *justified* in performing whatever music one desires. However, there are too many scenarios where this may be problematic: if, for example, a musician performs music meant for a funeral setting at a wedding. One can cause harm by not only checking who this music belongs to but, more importantly, who it serves. Therefore, I suggest an arrow that joins the "yes," after "Did I check?" to "Should it?" as this may encourage one to ponder ownership and how that informs them as a musician.

The second suggestion comes in the question, "Does it deserve mockery?" This may cause too much confusion as to what is entailed by the mockery. The term has too much derogatory meaning to be productive. This question would be more effective as "Does the music benefit from critique?" where a responder can engage better forms of analyses that the term critique encourages.

In order to "practice what I preach," I have completed the flow diagram for myself. Here, I am coming from the perspective of a Black African who composes and performs music largely using Euro-American Western traditions of music-making such as commercial popular music (hereafter, pop music). This is my process:

Question 1: "Do I claim it as my own?"
My response: "No"
Question 2: "Does it belong to or represent someone else?"
My response: "Yes" [Genres such as pop music stemmed out of the European and American technological advances that introduced electronic instruments, although the actual music (chords, rhythmic styles, etc.) borrows from many non-Western groups.]

Question 3: "Should it?"

My response: "Yes and No"

If "No":

Question 4: "Really?"

My response: "No" [Because commercial pop music has borrowed from so many different non-Western styles of music, it has become a neutral zone for many to express themselves, hence why the genre is so malleable and global in its reception]

Result: GO FOR IT!

If "Yes":

Question 4: "Do you respect or mock the community represented?"

My response: "Respect."

Question 5: "Would that community agree?"

My response: "Yes."

Question 6: "Is there a history of people being oppressed or exploited involved?"

My response: "Yes" [There are many songs that have borrowed from non-Western communities to gain success in the industry. However, when these communities produce their own music, they rarely garner the same level of international success (e.g., "One Dance" by Drake (Canadian) featuring Wizkid (Nigerian) and Kyla (British), which borrows heavily from the Caribbean dancehall style. As popular as dancehall is in the Caribbean, it gained notable reach through a Canadian rapper in the last decade. This can also be noted with the use of Latino styles to further Western artists; e.g., Justin Bieber in "Despacito.")][19]

Question 7: "Can I eventually contribute to undoing these systems of exploitation or ignorance as I play?"

My response: "Yes."

Question 8: "Have I had, or will I have, a relationship with the community represented?

My response: "Yes."

Result: GO FOR IT!

RESPONSE #5

Renata Yazzie
PhD Student in Ethnomusicology, Columbia University

Yá'át'ééh, shí éí Renata Yazzie yinishyé. Tó'aheedlíinii nishłį̨, Kinyaa'áanii báshíchíín, Bit'ahnii dashichei, Hónágháanii dashinálí—I greet you in this way, as a Diné woman. North American Indigenous songs have long been a source of inspiration for the colonial ear, where they form the backbone of modern-day ethnomusicology, to compositional inspiration and intent, where North American composers tried to use them for nationalistic purposes, and everything in between.

As one of a handful of Native musicologists, I am often asked some variation of: "My choir/ensemble would like to perform X piece by a white composer based on a traditional Navajo chant. Would this be appropriate?" It's always the same bastardized translation of one section of the Navajo Blessingway ceremony set to an equally awkward piece of music that tried to be Navajo-influenced. But the longer you listen to it, the more of a mockery it becomes. The answer for this scenario is *always* no.

But as more Indigenous composers emerge with critical and powerful works, sometimes the answer is a resounding yes![20] However sometimes, these pieces carry limitations. For example, Jacqueline Wilson, in her *Dance Suite for Solo Bassoon*, explicitly states that performers should research powwow music before playing the pieces and that they must not add "extramusical accompaniment" (read: drums and Native American flutes.)

All of these responses—no, maybe, and yes—are outlined nicely in Perman's chart, "Should I perform this music?" Perman's chart is not the end-all, but expertly sums up thinking points for engaging with music that is not of the performer's cultural or religious background. Understanding that the chart is not meant to be comprehensive, I recognize that it is primarily for the white undergraduate student encountering new works for the first time. For many, they have only taken one required ethnomusicology course and are fumbling for a more accurate sensitivity meter. This isn't necessarily a bad thing. The majority of students in North American music departments and conservatories are white and upper middle-class. If we are to grow a population of future music professionals who truly understand what intentional programming is, this is one place to start.

Intentional programming seeks to program musical works with care and thoughtfulness, from historically underrepresented communities, and is also intended to be a response to the rise of checkbox commissions and programming where underrepresented folks are included to check off a diversity box for funding or other incentives. Many larger music organizations and ensembles are working to diversify their repertoire. Yet even with good intentions, they still miss the mark, particularly with forming *and* sustaining community relationships. I appreciate that this chart highlights the necessity of forming community relationships, but anyone can attempt (or not attempt) forming a relationship with a community. When attempted, these relationships are often riddled with unspoken power dynamics and presented on one-sided terms. Thus, a healthy reciprocal relationship, as defined by the community's terms is important to keep at the forefront of the work and in truth, cannot be honestly answered for by the majority party. It is for this reason that I consider this chart a guide for white students, or students from privileged backgrounds, to consider their positionality as they decide what works to pursue in performance.

This begs the question whether this chart is even relevant or useful for students from historically underrepresented backgrounds? I went through this chart with a few pieces of my own choosing, the first being Ferruccio Busoni's *Indianisches Tagebuch I* (BV 267) which has a tagline of, "Vier Klavierstudien über Motive der R*thäute Amerikas." Most publishers kindly translate the German tagline as "Four studies on motifs of the North American Indians," but in reality, *rot* means "red" and *häute* means "skins." The four motifs represent songs from Hopi, Cheyenne, Akimel O'odham, and Wabanaki Nations. Do I claim it as my own? Definitely not. Does it belong to or represent someone else? Yes, it is meant to represent the aforementioned tribal nations to which I do not belong. But as one of those "North American Indians," the pieces might be ascribed to me. Should it? No, they are stolen and appropriated songs. Do I respect the community represented? Yes. Would that community agree? I hope so. Is there a history of people being oppressed? Yes. Can I eventually contribute to undoing these systems of exploitation or ignorance as I play? Here is where it gets dicey, because some people will say yes, and some people will say no. Am I going to pursue these pieces as an Indigenous person out of reclamation? Out of rematriation? At what point will I perform these?

Ultimately, this chart is great for white classical musicians to think through their privilege, the systemic inequalities that they benefit from, and what questions they should be asking themselves as they move beyond the standard Western European classical repertoire. Moreover, the chart remains somewhat useful in guiding a young person from a historically underrepresented group toward reflecting on their intent and purpose for performing certain works, but it is less direct with many extraneous questions to consider that aren't necessarily relevant. In this situation, I would ask first what the relationship is between a performer and their community, then consider intent, and decide thereafter. For many of our own communities, the well-being of the community precedes self-interests. Your answer, thus, lies in the relationship you have, and there isn't really a chart that can determine that for you.

POSTSCRIPT

Tony Perman

What a blessing it is to receive these words. I take them with humility and appreciation for the leap each author took to join this mini quest. I hesitate to take the last word, since I don't want to be your guide through the complexities my colleagues offer; that is for you to do. You have the next word. If so inclined, please take the chart, modify it, and make it yours (although keep in mind the ethics of acknowledgment implied in these essays as you do). As for me, my hope when I initiated this project was to be a better teacher, and I will surely benefit from the collective grace and wisdom of these voices for whom I have so much respect. In the spirit of Fred Moten and Stefano Harney, I am indebted.[21] At the very least, their thoughts confirm why seeking multiple perspectives is so invaluable!

In that spirit, I want to acknowledge some lessons I have received from each of my collaborators that I'll take with me into my next musical or teaching encounter. If this exercise has proven confounding, hopefully these words will invite you to revisit the chart, potentially create your own, and recognize the value of accepting multiple perspectives.

I admire Deborah Wong's joy in co-creation when the ethics of encounter are put front and center. She emphasizes the need for principled intent and good processes that resist a narrow emphasis on critique. But I especially appreciate her acknowledgment that the song she was moving to "contains the hope of social justice workers." This passing observation resonates with her career thus far, dedicated to arguing that principled scholars engaged in critical pedagogy can help identify the musical pathways of hope in "a time of trauma."[22]

I accept Danielle Brown's incisive insertion of asking "why" when engaging these decision-making processes.[23] More than anything, Dr. Brown's writing and pedagogy demonstrate the value of reflection. Understanding why and how musical choices are being made can, as she puts it, "serve as an entry point to learning about different people and cultures." Beyond her oft-cited challenge to music education's colonial complicity,[24] she demonstrates that love, reverence, respect for history, and wide-eyed clarity on one's own purpose can make each of us worthy ambassadors resisting the shadow of colonialism.[25]

I respect the stakes of these encounters exposed by Putu Hiranmayena for insiders whose livelihoods are often at the mercy of outside interest. While he aspires to shape students' "empathetic morals," he doesn't shy away from the reality that money is deeply involved. These potentially abstract questions have tangible consequences. As he says, there is "no separation of cultural arts from quotidian life." His writing reminds me of Jackson's acknowledgment that these acts of appropriation often leave people aggrieved.[26] Aspirations of utopia and the pain those dreams can cause show that "All of these elements of mainstream creativity push cultural and conceptual harm, which manifests in tangible social ills."[27] But as his addendum suggests, there is hope in fusing creativity and agency with respectful stewardship and curation.

I am inspired by Nkululeko Zungu's willingness to publicly take the plunge into the depths of the chart despite his credible critiques. I am thankful for his willingness to call out areas of concern. In particular, I take in his point that minimal reflection can make prospective musicians feel *justified* in their creative pursuits. Justification has been the cause of many ills and ought not be bestowed lightly. As a student and a composer balancing multiple identities, his embrace of the fact that this "should not be easy" and that musicians do not get to diminish music's complexity is important. Respectful creativity is hard work. His own music powerfully demonstrates this.[28]

I take stock of what a chart like this *can't* provide, as Renata Yazzie identifies by attending to the consequences of centering "I" at the expense of community and prioritizing "yes/no" at the expense of deeper reflection. More than anything, she reveals that the chart simply is not enough and serves some people more than others. Based on her thoughtful critique, what would such a chart look like if the relationship to the community came first? What would happen if the "I" was utterly erased and the potential for harm or "aggrievement" to the community was prioritized? A relationship isn't inevitably a good thing, and good intentions don't ensure success. She shares, perhaps, Paisley Rekdal's suggestion that risks can be worth taking if you're willing to listen and live with the consequences. As Yazzie has said elsewhere:

> Music is more than art; it defines our relationships as humans, to our world... studying new forms of listening and hearing, understanding how the senses work to input the sounds we make. These are all included within the possibilities of music.[29]

The most important questions don't have yes or no answers and the relationships that ought to form the center of these processes are always in formation, never fixed. Every line on the chart invites acknowledgments of ambiguity, contingency, and dynamism. A heuristic like this shouldn't placate the responsibilities of privilege nor invite secure resolution. After all, there's likely never a final "Yes" at the end of "Go For It!"

But now that you are at the end, I hope you recognize that all of these questions have people and relationships at their center. When you make music for others or by others, when you share music with others, or even listen to music from others, you are entering into a relationship with them and contributing to the history of those sounds. If you acknowledge that music's value emerges from its context and if you hope that your musicality can make the world a better place, then, I would argue, cultivating those relationships, acknowledging the people who make your engagement possible, and recognizing your own potential complicity in the dynamics that make these questions matter is the place to start.

Chimamanda Ngozi Adichie's warning against "The Danger of a Single Story" resonates with the issues we confront here.[30] Too often, privileged musicians who engage these questions of appropriation seek a single story or solution. They either treat all performance across difference as cultural appropriation or protect all artistic exploration as demonstrations of freedom: end of story. Narrow perspectives such as this do a disservice to human complexity and dynamism, to say nothing of the inevitability that musical interaction will either undermine or reinforce social inequality. In music, the risks and rewards are vast. I admire Dylan Robinson and Patrick Nickleson's argument that, "Our relationships to music can be, if we let them, practical training in learning to feel and know the possibility of other ways of relating."[31] The next step is for each of us to make our own musical choices as members of dynamic communities, listen well, and reflect on how our choices impact others and contribute (or not) to the world in which we aspire to live.

GLOSSARY

Tony Perman

Acknowledgment

Cultural appropriation and academic honesty function similarly. Too often, academic honesty is framed in litigious terms instead of moral ones. Students avoid the moving target of plagiarism out of fear of the consequences and focus on the legal ramifications of appropriation more than the moral risks or the intellectual value in acknowledging influence and crediting sources. Centering mutuality and acknowledgment for students dipping their toe in the long-running waters of academic inquiry puts intellectual history first and honors the work that has already been done. It helps shape the academic community and welcomes students into the conversation. In publications, the beginning and the end of the text are often gestures at intellectual honesty, obligation, and potential community in the acknowledgments section and the bibliography of works cited. Our citations gesture at the long-standing and ongoing academic conversations we are entering and each of our respective intellectual journeys both in and out of the academy.

The peer review process itself also contributes to this sense of obligation and these flowing conversations. They aren't exactly mutual, since none of us writing here know who our reviewers were, but our two peer reviewers and team of student reviewers for *Open Access Musicology* have all strengthened this article immensely. It might be productive, for the sake of transparency and in the spirit of this essay, to acknowledge a few of their suggestions here and the ways in which we have chosen to respond to them. At their suggestion, we contextualized this work in the scholarship on cultural appropriation more explicitly and tried to guide student readers with more preparatory material but without dictating what is "right." I've also defined the more abstract terms that matter like "freedom" and "empathy." The area of greatest divergence has to do with the chart itself. One reviewer worried that the chart might be too confusing, too busy, and potentially neglectful of numerous gray areas. That reviewer suggested I simplify it and be more explicit about its value. Because this is the chart my colleagues were asked to engage with, I decided to leave it as is, but I certainly acknowledge that reviewer's concerns. If it seems too difficult or implies clear-cut answers to complex ethical questions, I invite you to design your own. I think the chart has value because it forces users to confront those gray areas and acknowledge a broad array of potential considerations without evading the decision-making process. Critique needs action to be productive, even if the accompanying action is refusal. But it can be easy to focus too much on the yes/no nature of the questions, which I think many of my colleagues here rightfully call out. Every instance will differ. As you read, consider what questions matter most? How do you reconcile general questions about cultural appropriation with the instance-specific evaluations creative people hopefully confront every day?

Finally, in the spirit of acknowledgment, I want to thank all my coauthors for being willing to take this path, the editors and reviewers of *Open Access Musicology* for their guidance, and the many, many students who've taught me how to think better over the years.

Community

You are likely a member of countless communities. You don't need the humanities or social sciences to know that. But defining community is surprisingly tricky and has been done many times in many disciplines. Community can operate as a "mode of experience," as an "affective assemblage," or beyond our everyday encounters in the form of "imagined communities."[32] I hesitate to impose my own definition since I recognize that I think like an ethnomusicologist socialized as a white, male, agnostic, middle-class US citizen, but for the sake of transparency, I define community as "the composite relations grounded in similarity and difference among agents who act on their interdependence or mutual indebtedness."[33] I've learned to put the sense of indebtedness at the center of this definition, and indeed as a driving principle of my own social life from the theorists Fred Moten and Stefano Harney.[34] The three key features of community are that members: a) recognize that they are similar to one another; b) recognize that they are distinct from others; and c) feel indebted to one another.

Cultural Appropriation

Appropriation vs. appreciation. Appropriation vs. theft. Appropriation vs. misappropriation. These are the binaries my students usually raise in class. In critical scholarship and popular discourse, cultural appropriation often focuses on problematic instances that lead to negative consequences.[35] Existing approaches to cultural appropriation are not always well-suited to understanding the countless cross-cultural interactions that raise significant ethical issues and questions of contested meaning. While deeply meaningful, music's meaning (as in the relationship between what sounds represent and the effects that those representations have) is unpredictable because it emerges from the ways in which people engage with it and with one another. Music's consistent ability to elicit emotional responses in listeners and performers make the meanings generated musically both visceral and personal. I hope the chart here helps capture instances during which performers knowingly cross boundaries of identity or community in ways that are ethically ambiguous but have both positive and negative potential outcomes.

The poet and essayist Paisley Rekdal defines appropriation as "the use of a preexisting object or image that you've repurposed without fundamentally changing it."[36] Her book is remarkable, but the conclusions she draws are also primarily relevant to literary appropriation and creative writing. Writing from the perspective of a character with a different identity than the author raises a different set of questions than performing music associated with communities other than one's own. The role of creativity complicates things further. Jason Baird Jackson, as a folklorist, distinguishes appropriation from analogous processes like diffusion, acculturation, and assimilation.[37] He sees appropriation as an inversion of assimilation in which appropriation is the "unidirectional taking of cultural forms from a subordinate group by members of a dominant group, aggrieving members of the subordinate group."[38] One only has to consider the harm appropriation has done within Indigenous and African American communities in the United State to recognize how much weight this word "aggrieved" ought to carry in these evaluations.

While every term is open to interpretation, if something musical matters to someone other than you, their status as marginalized or not must be taken into consideration. The impact of your engagement is not incidental. If you or I want to engage with that music, perhaps even just as a listener, our relationship to them and the community in which it matters is as important to consider as their perspective on our engagement. I tell my mbira students that it is unreasonable to expect them to have a relationship with the Shona community to whom it matters so much from the moment they walk in the door. But I also tell them that if they want to continue making mbira music a part of their life, they should probably foster those relationships and ensure that their participation doesn't perpetuate the global systems of inequity that shape Zimbabwe's global positionality or "aggrieve" members of that community. Matthew Morrison's concept of "Blacksound" captures just how deeply centuries of exploitation of Black expressive practices have shaped cultural life in the United States. He explores it in order to "trace the musical, political, structural, and proprietary legacies of blackface minstrelsy—a theatrical form that emerged during slavery as the nation's *first* original mass entertainment."[39] In other words, popular culture in the US has its origins in years of unfettered cultural appropriation.

But borrowing needn't be so grim. Rekdal ultimately concludes with a hopeful consideration of the risk/reward negotiation that any creative person must confront. While appropriation risks reinforcing racism or eroding legitimate claims of authority or agency, it can also resist those possibilities and open new pathways of connection and community by requiring us to interrogate historically enmeshed relationships.[40] In this regard, she reaches similar conclusions to the philosopher Kathleen Higgins in her quest for ethical musical practice and education.[41] Further, Rekdal pushes students to acknowledge that there are no shortcuts.

Compassion, curiosity, respect and creativity are all worth pursuing.[42] But you must also accept that mistakes can happen and be ready to accept the consequences.

Decolonization

Colonization remade the world, consolidating power in the service of white supremacy and causing unfathomable harm across the globe. Decolonization was initially about undoing that process and returning sovereignty to formerly subjugated peoples. But it remained incomplete, since so many of the structures of colonialism remained in place. In North America, for example, land was never returned to displaced Indigenous people. Decolonization is now also about reshaping social theory and higher education in ways that are both radical yet woefully incomplete. Decoloniality has come to refer to a new kind of thought and practice focused on untangling the roots of settler colonialism in every facet of life, demanding accountability, redress, and recognition of the cost of history. The goals of decolonization include social and epistemic justice, through a "radical transformation in relations of power, worldviews, and, in an academic context, our role as scholars and our relationship to the university as an industry."[43] The specifics differ depending on which colonial history you are working to undo. For example, the legacies of racism, chattel slavery, and the disruptions to Indigenous communities caused by settler colonialism operate very differently in Zimbabwe than in Iowa, the two places I work and live. What is shared, however, are the privileges inherited from white supremacy. My subjectivity in both places is shaped by these privileges and entangled in these histories in ways that inevitably inform my musical interactions and choices.

Understanding music in places affected by colonialism (which is most of the globe) is incomplete without centering Indigenous agency and priorities. Recent scholars often emphasize how decolonizing history, theory, or music studies might shape that understanding and prioritize substantive redress.[44] However, the philosopher Olúfẹ́mi Táíwò rejects this project of decolonization, arguing that its impulse to purge all evidence of the colonial past from formerly colonized spaces undermines African agency. Rather, it performs a gesture of moral authenticity on the part of the concerned author, perhaps begging the question "Should I perform this theory?"[45]

Similarly, Tuck and Yang are wary of metaphorical acts of redress because they are evasive, defer real change, and return whiteness to the center.[46] Redress needs to be structural and substantive, not additive. In higher education, redress can take the form of making curricular space for previously ignored disciplines, theories, and bodies of knowledge by moving Eurocentric bodies of knowledge out from the centers of those disciplines. Simply adding diversity to Eurocentric centers falls short. Redress can also involve refusal, whether on the part of Indigenous actors refusing to conform to the expectations bestowed upon them, or potential subjects refusing to be complicit in processes that maintain any colonial-era status quo, or beyond. For Tuck and Yang,

> Refusal, and stances of refusal in research, are attempts to place limits on conquest and the colonization of knowledge by marking what is off limits, what is not up for grabs or discussion, what is sacred, and what can't be known.[47]

Honoring these stances of refusal can dramatically influence the potential performances and musical spaces you have in mind as you consider this chart and the potential for cultural appropriation. Redress can also mean listening to (and hiring!) voices whose wisdom has been ignored, either because they aren't credentialed in the same way or because the foundation of their knowledge doesn't fit the boxes celebrated in colonized spaces. I, for instance, acknowledge that the spirits for whom the mbira is played, while being valued actors in Shona ceremonial life, are also theorists, just as much as the living Zimbabwean scholars who shape the way music and life there is understood.

Making collaborative space for my coauthors here who identify, at least partially, with Bali, South Africa, the African diaspora, East Asia, and the Diné Nation, with minimal editorial oversight is one small way I am working to decenter my own colonial privilege. I put these explanatory paragraphs at the end of this article as a small step toward mitigating the centrality of my own voice. Their voices are also essential since, as Yazzie points out in her response, the chart likely speaks more to white students than anyone else. On the one hand, this reflects my own identity and its accompanying biases. On the other hand, those who have acquired privilege as "members of a dominant group" are more prone to "aggrieving members of subordinate groups."[48] We are, perhaps, more in need of tools to guide ethical practice. But that is for you to decide. Epistemic freedom depends on the relationships that emerge in scholarship, music-making, and listening being acknowledged, equitable, and engaged with humility and a recognition of mutual indebtedness. It depends on acknowledging harm and accepting accountability. My hope is that by centering the questions asked in this chart in curricular spaces we can eventually diversify the curriculum itself, center marginalized voices in and out of the classroom, and contribute to more substantive structural change. For Táíwò, labeling these intellectually and morally sound practices reductively as "decolonization" may actually entrench colonial history and perform morality at the expense of Indigenous agency or substantive redress, but as I (along with Stefan Fiol) have written elsewhere:

> Decolonizing music studies involves acts of refusal and disengagement as well as an antiracist commitment to lay bare our disciplinary habits of body and mind. [...] As a community of scholars that has worked to elucidate the music/community relationship for many years, it is critical to address how the social dynamics that [we] study can be more equitably reflected in the institutions, practices, and interpersonal dynamics that define us.[49]

Empathy

At first glance, empathy is an inherent good, regardless of which of the many definitions you might encounter. Lay definitions connect the English word "empathy" to an ability to share or understand the feelings of another. After a long discussion of what it means to walk in "someone else's shoes," the primatologist Franz de Waal defines empathy as, "the capacity to (a) be affected by and share the emotional state of another, (b) assess the reasons for the other's state, and (c) identify with the other, adopting his or her perspective."[50] The philosopher Kathleen Higgins identifies the capacity for empathy as an essential peace-building skill and advocates for music that cultivates this capacity. She urges educators to embrace music's ability to generate empathy as a strategy toward contributing to, "a more harmonious and peaceful world."[51]

This all seems potentially beautiful, but there are risks. Saidiya Hartman presents a powerful example in which a white anti-slavery activist's effort to empathize with the enslaved in the nineteenth century United States ultimately erased the agency and subjectivity of the very people he was trying to understand. For Hartman

> [...] the repressive effects of empathy—can be located in the "obliteration of otherness" or the facile intimacy that enables identification with the other only as we "feel ourselves into those we imagine as ourselves." And as a result, empathy fails to expand the space of the other but merely places the self in its stead.[52]

For Hartman, empathy, as the "projection of oneself into another to better understand the other" is precarious.[53] Potential empathizers risk shifting from witness to spectator. To resist just such an ego-driven imposition, the writer Namwali Serpell urges the idea of "visiting" the other as a guest rather than as an empath. For Serpell, "Empathy is, in a word, selfish."[54] She recommends the distance inherent in representation (as suggested by Hannah Arendt) as an alternative to empathy.[55] The writer Paisley Rekdal ultimately agrees, saying that "Empathy may be a profound, exciting, and beneficial emotion, but it cannot be used to justify or critically frame any work engaged in appropriation."[56] When musicking with others (or in relation to others), it is an open question for each of you to consider how the emotional connections shaped through shared experience can generate either side of empathy—as a positive means of understanding human difference or as a voyeuristic exploitation of another's experience. There is no obvious or single answer.

Ensembles

Following Mantle Hood's guidance at UCLA, the emergence of ethnomusicology as an established perspective on music education brought with it "world music" ensembles.[57] These ensembles, often from Southeast Asia or Africa, were meant to offer alternatives to the typical collegiate musical ensembles rooted in Western European art music, but they often followed a similar format culminating in staged performances at the end of every semester. As a paradigm for music education, ethnomusicology is built on a paradox between its advocacy for context as the bedrock of musical meaning and its advocacy for decontextualized ensembles as the most productive space for embodied learning. There has been a lot written recently about the value of these ensembles as well as the potential risks.[58] Further, as David Locke points out from his perspective as the director of an ensemble of Ghanaian music:

> The study and performance of African music in the United States might seem to be an apolitical activity that is focused on making good music, learning about unfamiliar music-cultures, and fostering international good will. But global relations of power and issues of social justice simmer beneath the optimistic humanistic surface.[59]

I teach a Zimbabwean mbira ensemble and have come to value it as my most important teaching space. In comparison to reading, listening, and discussing music, the embodied learning that takes place in participatory settings such as this are the most powerful pedagogical spaces I know. They are invaluable. Yet it is undeniable that the classroom in which I teach it to predominantly inexperienced new musicians has separated the music from its context. In Zimbabwe, the mbira is usually played for spirits in conjunction with dance, beer, snuff, and public gathering with a clear division of labor. Mbira players provide a service: they aren't performing for others' entertainment. The pressure from universities to publicly perform has long been a source of tension for many ensemble directors, musicians, and insider musical ambassadors.[60] While my teachers and interlocutors in Zimbabwe support what I do, there is more than one point of view. One commentator from Zimbabwe describes performers like me as "white vampires" exploiting Zimbabwe's music.[61] Navigating these disagreements is a never-ending process. This chart might help you resolve this paradox and render risky engagements with others in contexts of structural inequality helpful rather than harmful, but it won't always. Musical encounters can be attentive to mutual indebtedness, recognize communities who are oppressed and marginalized, and recognize that sustained musical engagement has the potential to help alleviate that oppression or marginalization by including relationships of mutual understanding.

Freedom

In my article on the ethical quandaries that emerge when North Americans play the mbira, I wrote the following:

> Freedom is such a slippery word. Used widely, it is hard to separate from the assumptions or values of its user, ever tied to secularism, liberalism, and political sovereignty. For the mbira, freedom can't be fully secular without erasing its spiritual foundations. It can't be liberal without imposing attitudes about freedom tied to the "West" and neoliberalism. What are the consequences of musical freedom or the dangers of experiential schizophonia? This species of schizophonia detaches the sonic from the social, separates potential signs from long-established semiotic objects, and reimagines sounds to reflect the new performers' values.[62]

When playing or performing music associated with someone other than oneself, there is a precarious tension between creatively expressing one's own experience versus respectfully acknowledging the authorities to whom the music in question is beholden. Schizophonia detaches sounds from their source.[63] While Schafer was thinking of recordings, the term has utility in contexts like "world music ensembles" as well. Kyra Gaunt describes a very similar process as "context collapse" in her critique of Miley Cyrus's appropriation of twerking in which diverse audiences are flattened into a single context.[64] When initially learning new music, learners inevitably mimic their teachers or guides. This "mimesis," for the anthropologist Michael Taussig, can be a mode of becoming other.[65] Schizophonia seemingly encourages a kind of artistic freedom that removes the specter of responsibility because sound has been detached from its source or its context. But such "freedom" risks enabling the kind of voyeuristic empathy that Saidiya Hartman so powerfully cautions against.[66] If your freedom risks erasing the lived experience of the other, you have caused harm and ignored the sense of indebtedness to the community for whom the music you have engaged matters. But freedom's relationship to the rights our heritage grants us is complex. Achille Mbembe asks, "what is freedom if one cannot really break with this accident of being born somewhere—the relation of flesh and bones, the double law of soil and blood?"[67]

Mutual Obligation

I see mutual obligation as one of the central tenets of community. My approach has emerged from thinking with my colleague Stefan Fiol and was inspired by the writing of Stefano Harney and Fred Moten about the idea of debt.[68] Mutual indebtedness would be a more accurate phrase. For them, debt is productive when activated as a principle of social life acquired through interaction and historical inheritance.[69] It must be acknowledged, is always mutual,[70] and most importantly, can never be repaid or forgiven.[71] I value the idea of debt and mutual obligation because it seems a path toward generating a sense of community that isn't utopian and doesn't overlook the inequities of history. In their ever-opaque prose, they write:

> There is this debt at a distance to a global politics of blackness emerging out of slavery and colonialism, a black radical politics, a politics of debt

> without payment, without credit, without limit. This debt was built in a struggle with empire before empire, where power was not with institutions or governments alone, where any owner or colonizer had the violent power of a ubiquitous state.[72]

Without this acknowledgment of mutual obligation or indebtedness, community is difficult to achieve.

Mutual obligation can also productively serve two other conversations that ought to accompany all humanistic inquiry on North American university campuses: land acknowledgments and academic honesty. Land acknowledgments have increased in frequency in recent years, first in Canada and then the United States. On the positive side, more and more teachers, researchers, and administrators recognize that ignoring the history of the land where they are teaching their classes, conducting their research, or housing their institutions is a problem, discursively erasing the Indigenous communities living around them. Acknowledging this brings attention to what has historically been ignored.[73] On the other hand, unless it is accompanied by active redress and return, oft-repeated acknowledgments can feel hollow, insincere, and self-serving. As I grapple with their value in my own work, I reflect on the point of acknowledgment through Harney and Moten's concept of debt and the necessity to center mutual obligation in community. As a member of my own community in Iowa, just down the road from the Meskwaki settlement, my actions here will guide whether I am justified or worthy of making such an acknowledgment as a step in repaying my own unpayable debt.[74] A consideration of mutual obligation can also clarify considerations of academic honesty (see "Acknowledgment").

Performance

As someone who prioritizes participatory music and music for personal growth and edification, I don't limit the idea of performance to music that is staged for others. I've long admired Christopher Small's definition of musicking when he says, "To music is to take part, in any capacity, in a musical performance"[75] and use it as the basis for my own thinking in these regards. I hope the term can include the high-level distinctions some of you might make between Aristotelian poiesis and praxis, while also accommodating the inclusive participatory sonic experiences of ceremonial and collective events common throughout the world. Obviously, questions of ethics present themselves differently depending on if others are listening and who those others are, but even passively listening to something on Spotify or YouTube has ethical implications. I would recommend going through the chart with a very specific potential experience of playing, performing, practicing, or even listening in mind. How do different ideas of "performance" change the path you navigate?

NOTES

1. Danielle Brown was also invited to participate in this collective essay. Her published response can be found on her own website: Danielle Brown, "Should I Perform This Music?" My People Tell Stories, accessed September 11, 2024, https://www.mypeopletellstories.com/should-i-perform-this-music.
2. Each of the terms in **bold** throughout this opening section appear in the glossary at the end of the article. While none of these explanations is intended to be definitive, reflecting on what each term means for you in relation to how I (Tony Perman) thought about them as I designed the chart and solicited reactions from colleagues should hopefully be productive. This glossary includes *acknowledgment*, *community*, *cultural appropriation*, *decolonization*, *empathy*, *ensembles*, *freedom*, *mutual obligation*, and *performance*. Thus, please see the glossary for more discussion of *cultural appropriation*.
3. The mbira (also known as *nhare* or *mbira dzavadzimu*) is the most widely heard of several related instruments from Zimbabwe with metal keys struck by a player's thumbs and forefingers. Beyond some structural similarities, the purposes with which these instruments are played, core repertoire, and expectations of performance vary from one instrument to the next. The mbira I teach is primarily played in ceremonies in Shona communities during which during which the spirits of the dead enter the bodies of host mediums as one component of vibrant multisensory events. While there were very few players during the early decades of the twentieth century (at the height of British colonialism), by 2025 there were hundreds of players in

Zimbabwe and in multiple countries around the world in a robust interconnected community organized around this sacred musical tradition and its homeland. There are numerous references to mbira music in Zimbabwe, but a good starting point includes Perminus Matiure. "Mbira Dzavadzimu and Its Space within the Shona Cosmology: Tracing *Mbira* from *Bira* to the Spiritual World." *Muziki: Journal of Music Research in Africa* 8, no. 2 (2011): 29–49; Tute Wincil Chigamba and Jennifer Kyker. *Sekuru's Stories* (2019), https://sekuru.org; Tony Perman, "Love and Debt: Performing Difference on the Mbira," in *Music Making Community*, eds. Tony Perman and Stefan Fiol, (University of Illinois Press, 2024), 209–31.

4. Danielle Brown, "An Open Letter on Racism in Music Studies: Especially Ethnomusicology and Music Education," My People Tell Stories, June 12, 2020, https://www.mypeopletellstories.com/blog/open-letter.
5. Dylan Robinson, *Hungry Listening: Resonant Theory for Indigenous Studies* (University of Minnesota Press, 2020).
6. Eve Tuck and K. Wayne Yang, "Decolonization is Not a Metaphor," *Decolonization: Indigeneity, Education & Society* 1, no. 1 (2012): 1–40.
7. Perman, "Love and Debt."
8. Banjo studies is an ever-expanding field, but the following provide an excellent starting point: Laurent Dubois. *The Banjo: America's African Instrument* (Belknap Press, 2016); The Great Courses, "Uncovering the History of the Banjo with Rhiannon Giddens," YouTube, March 23, 2023, educational video, https://www.youtube.com/watch?v=RiP8Tfa8bB8; Matthew D. Morrison. *Blacksound: Making Race and Popular Music in the United States* (Oakland, CA: University of California Press, 2024).
9. Eric Lott, *Love and Theft: Blackface Minstrelsy and the American Working Class,* (Oxford University Press, 1993).
10. Dylan Robinson and Patrick Nickleson, "The Feeling of Knowing Music," in *The Affect Theory Reader 2: Worldings, Tensions, Futures*, eds. Gregory J. Seigworth and Carolyn Pedwell (Duke University Press, 2023), 289.
11. Robinson and Nickleson, "Feeling of Knowing Music," 286.
12. Robinson and Nickleson, "Feeling of Knowing Music," 287.
13. Kathleen Marie Higgins, "Connecting Music to Ethics," *College Music Symposium* 58, no. 3 (2018): 1–20.
14. Paisley Rekdal. *Appropriate: A Provocation* (W.W. Norton, 2021), 190.
15. You can hear the song and view a dance tutorial of it on YouTube (Great Leap, Inc., "Bambutsu for Tsuru For Solidarity," YouTube, June 23, 2020, educational video, https://www.youtube.com/watch?v=24FEYJYTknQ), produced in 2020 during the pandemic. Take a look at a five-minute documentary

about it (Great Leap, Inc., "Great Leap – FandangObon Short Documentary," YouTube, February 6, 2014, educational video, https://www.youtube.com/watch?v=bPwaYvXH_gw), made and produced in 2013 by Great Leap, Nobuko Miyamoto's nonprofit arts organization.

16. For more information, see Nobuko Miyamoto, *120,000 Stories*, Smithsonian Folkways Recordings SFW 40590, Asian Pacific America Series, 2021, compact disc; Nobuko Miyamoto, *Not Yo' Butterfly: My Long Song of Relocation, Race, Love, and Revolution*, eds. Deborah Wong (University of California Press, 2021); George Lipsitz, "'Welcome to the Dance': FandangObon as a Polycultural Anti-Racist Remix," in *Rebel Musics, Volume 2: Human Rights, Resistant Sounds, and the Politics of Music Making*, eds. Daniel Fischlin and Ajay Heble, 129–47 (Black Rose Books, 2020); Sojin Kim, "Just Dance: Connecting Life, Death, Traditions, and Communities in L.A.," Folklife Magazine, Smithsonian Center for Folklife and Cultural Heritage, August 25, 2014, https://folklife.si.edu/talkstory/2014/just-dance-connecting-life-death-traditions-and-communities-in-l-a.
17. Martha Gonzalez, *Chican@ Artivistas: Music, Community, and Transborder Tactics in East Los Angeles* (University of Texas Press, 2020), 91.
18. Homi K. Bhabha, *The Location of Culture* (Routledge, 1994).
19. See Bruce Ziff and Pratima V. Rao, "Introduction to Cultural Appropriation: A Framework for Analysis," in *Borrowed Power: Essays on Cultural Appropriation*, eds. Bruce Ziff and Pratima V. Rao (Rutgers University Press, 1997), 1–23.
20. See works for solo piano by Charles Shadle (Choctaw), "Choctaw Animals: Four Not-Too-Difficult Pieces for Piano"; Beverley McKiver's (Anishinaabe) pieces for solo piano, "Canadian Floral Emblems Suite"; and various chamber and instrumental works by Raven Chacon (Diné).
21. Stefano Harney and Fred Moten, *The Undercommons: Fugitive Planning and Black Study* (Minor Compositions, 2013).
22. Deborah Wong, "An Ethnomusicology of Hope in a Time of Trauma," in *Musical Islands: Exploring Connections Between Music, Place, and Research,* eds. Elizabeth Mackinlay, Brydie-Leigh Bartleet, and Katelyn Barney (Cambridge Scholars Publishing, 2009), 3–19.
23. Brown, "Should I Perform This Music?"
24. Brown, "Open Letter on Racism in Music Studies."
25. Danielle Brown, *East of Flatbush, North of Love: An Ethnography of Home* (My People Tell Stories, LLC., 2015).
26. Jason Baird Jackson, "On Cultural Appropriation," *Journal of Folklore Research* 58, no. 1 (2021): 77–122.

27. Putu Tangkas Adi Hiranmayena and Elizabeth McLean Macy, "Passing the Mic from White Middle-Aged Spiritual Liberation to Post-College Travel Utopia," The Collective, February 16, 2023, https://thecollectiveis.us/?p=6080.
28. Dancz Center for New Music at UGA, "Composition Recital—Nkululeko Zungu," YouTube, April 18, 2024, https://www.youtube.com/watch?v=DvgoN5JDQto.
29. This quote is cited in Maya Cunningham, Dylan Robinson, Chris Stover, Leslie Tilley, and Anna Yu Wang, "Introduction: Beyond Western Musicalities," *Engaging Students: Essays in Music Pedagogy* 8 (February 2022).
30. Chimamanda Ngozi Adichie, "The Danger of a Single Story," TED Talk, July 2009, https://www.ted.com/talks/chimamanda_ngozi_adichie_the_danger_of_a_single_story.
31. Robinson and Nickleson, "Feeling of Knowing Music," 291.
32. Community as a "mode of experience" comes from Anthony P. Cohen, *Symbolic Construction of Community* (Tavistock Productions, 1985); "affective assemblages" from Gilles Deleuze and Felix Guattari, *A Thousand Plateaus: Capitalism and Schizophrenia*, transl. Brian Massumi (University of Minnesota Press, 1987); and "imagined communities" from Benedict Anderson, *Imagined Communities: Reflections on the Origin and Spread of Nationalism* (Verso, 1983).
33. Stefan Fiol and Tony Perman, "Introduction: Music Making (and Unmaking) Community," in *Music Making Community*, eds. Tony Perman and Stefan Fiol (University of Illinois Press, 2024), 8.
34. Harney and Moten, *The Undercommons*.
35. There are too many influential texts to fully capture here, but there are several useful places to start, particularly Rekdal, *Appropriate*; and Jackson, "On Cultural Appropriation"; but also James O. Young, *Cultural Appropriation and the Arts* (Blackwell Publishing, 2008); Jessica Andrews, Renee Cox, and Matthew D. Morrison, "Culture Now: Appreciate/Appropriate: Panel Discussion," in *Culture as Catalyst*, ed. Isolde Brielmaier, 210–223 (Frances Young Tang Teaching Museum and Art Gallery at Skidmore College, 2020).
36. Rekdal, *Appropriate*, 18.
37. Jackson, "On Cultural Appropriation."
38. Jackson, "On Cultural Appropriation," 89.
39. Morrison, "Blacksound," 2.
40. Rekdal, *Appropriate*, 190.
41. Higgins, "Connecting Music to Ethics."
42. Rekdal, *Appropriate*.

43. Luis Chávez and Russell P. Skelchy, "Decolonization for Ethnomusicology and Music Studies in Higher Education," *Action, Criticism, and Theory for Music Education* 18, no. 3 (2019): 115.
44. There is a lot written about decolonization in music studies. See Chávez and Skelchy, "Decolonization for Ethnomusicology"; Brown, "Open Letter on Racism"; Robinson, *Hungry Listening*. For more on decolonization and social theory from the perspective of the Global South, see Sabelo J. Ndlovu-Gatsheni, *Epistemic Freedom in Africa: Deprovincialization and Decolonization* (Routledge, 2018); Silvia Rivera Cusicanqui, *Ch'ixinakax Utxiwa: On Practices and Discourses of Decolonization*, transl. Molly Geidel (Polity Press, 2020); Achille Mbembe, *Out of the Dark Night: Essays on Decolonization* (Columbia University Press, 2021).
45. Olúfẹ́mi Táíwò, *Against Decolonisation: Taking African Agency Seriously* (Hurst Publishers, 2022), 4.
46. Tuck and Yang, "Decolonization is not a Metaphor."
47. Eve Tuck and K. Wayne Yang, "R-Words: Refusing Research," in *Humanizing Research: Decolonizing Qualitative Inquiry with Youth and Communities*, eds. Django Paris and Maisha T. Winn (Sage, 2014), 225.
48. Jackson, "On Cultural Appropriation," 89.
49. Fiol and Perman, "Introduction," 13.
50. Frans B. M. de Waal, "Putting the Altruism Back into Altruism: The Evolution of Empathy," *Annual Review of Psychology* 59 (2008): 281.
51. Higgins, "Connecting Music to Ethics," 8.
52. Saidiya V. Hartman, *Scenes of Subjection: Terror, Slavery, and Self-Making in Nineteenth-Century America* (W.W. Norton, 2022), 26.
53. Hartman, *Scenes of Subjection*, 24.
54. Namwali Serpell, "The Banality of Empathy," *New York Review of Books*, March 2, 2019, https://hcommons.org/app/uploads/sites/1002235/2021/03/The-Banality-of-Empathy-by-Namwali-Serpell-The-New-York-Review-of-Books.pdf
55. Serpell, "Banality of Empathy."
56. Rekdal, *Appropriate*, 54.
57. See Mantle Hood, "The Challenge of 'Bi-Musicality'," *Ethnomusicology* 4, no. 2 (1960): 55–59; Chávez and Skelchy, "Decolonization for Ethnomusicology."
58. See Ted Solis, ed., *Performing Ethnomusicology: Teaching and Representation in World Music Ensembles* (University of California Press, 2004); Elizabeth A. Clendinning, *American Gamelan and the Ethnomusicological Imagination* (University of Illinois Press, 2020); Juliet Hess, "Performing the 'Exotic?':

Constructing an Ethical World Music Ensemble," *Visions of Research in Music Education* 23 (2013); Perman, "Love and Debt."

59. David Locke, "The African Ensemble in America: Contradictions and Possibilities," in *Performing Ethnomusicology*, ed. Solis, 168–88, 168.
60. Roger Vetter, "A Square Peg in a Round Hole: Teaching Javanese Gamelan in the Ensemble Paradigm of the Academy," in *Performing Ethnomusicology*, ed. Solis, 115–25.
61. Tanyaradzwa Tawengwa, "Cultural Vampires: White Exploitation of Zimbabwean Mbira Music," *Daily News,* May 26, 2020, https://dailynews.co.zw/cultural-vampires-white-exploitation-of-zimbabwean-mbira-music/.
62. Perman, "Love and Debt," 219.
63. R. Murray Schafer, *The Tuning of the World* (Random House, 1977).
64. Kyra D. Gaunt, "YouTube, Twerking & You: Context Collapse and the Handheld Co-presence of Black Girls and Miley Cyrus," *Journal of Popular Music Studies* 27, no. 3, (2015): 244–273.
65. Michael Taussig, *Mimesis and Alterity: A Particular History of the Senses* (Routledge, 1993).
66. Hartman, *Scenes of Subjection.*
67. Mbembe, *Out of the Dark Night*, 185
68. Harney and Moten, *The Undercommons*; Fiol and Perman, "Introduction."
69. Harney and Moten, *The Undercommons*, 154-159.
70. Harney and Moten, *The Undercommons*, 61.
71. Harney and Moten, *The Undercommons*, 63.
72. Harney and Moten, *The Undercommons*, 64.
73. Dylan Robinson, Kanonhsyonne Janice C. Hill, Armand Garnet Ruffo, Selena Coutoure, and Lisa Cooke Ravensbergen, "Rethinking the Practice and Performance of Indigenous Land Acknowledgment," *Canadian Theatre Review* 177 (2019): 20–30.
74. Harney and Moten, *The Undercommons*, 63.
75. Christopher Small, "Musicking—The Meanings of Performing and Listening. A Lecture," *Music Education Research* 1, no. 1 (1999): 12.